CURING THE MISCHIEFS OF FACTION

Party Reform in America

JEFFERSON MEMORIAL LECTURES

Curing the
Mischiefs of Faction
Party Reform in America

AUSTIN RANNEY

University of California Press

Berkeley, Los Angeles, London

University of California Press
Berkeley and Los Angeles, California
University of California Press, Ltd.
London, England

First Paperback Edition, 1976
ISBN: 0-520-03215-2
Library of Congress Catalog Card Number: 73-90657
Printed in the United States of America

TO JAY, DOUGLAS, GORDON, AND DAVID

"Whom should a son bear with, if not his own father?"
TERENCE, *The Self Tormentor*, I, 111

Contents

Preface

This book began as the Jefferson Memorial Lectures, given at the University of California, Berkeley in February and March of 1973. Since its present structure differs considerably from what I first intended, perhaps its evolution is worth recounting briefly.

Chancellor Albert H. Bowker's invitation specified only that the lectures be "broadly concerned with the principles of American democracy and the form of American government as conceived by the fathers of the Constitution. . . or with the development of their ideas in later periods." At the time the invitation arrived I was a member of the Democratic party's Commission on Party Structure and Delegate Selection (the "McGovern-Fraser commission") and much involved in its reforms of the party's rules for choosing national convention delegates. I was and am also a political scientist whose scholarly attention has long been focused on the organization and role of political parties in democratic government. As both participant and observer I sought to understand the cognitions and values underlying the arguments made both for and against our reforms; and since the commission was discharged in 1972 I have tried to identify and evaluate the impact of the reforms on the party and the nation. It therefore seemed both appropriate and timely to accept Nelson Polsby's suggestion that I present an account of the theory and practice of party reform throughout American history; and

it appeared reasonable to offer it in the form of a chronological narrative beginning with the demise of presidential
nominations by congressional caucuses in the 1820s and
ending with the McGovern-Fraser rules in the 1970s.

However, the more I learned about the issues and forces
involved in earlier efforts at reform the more I was struck
by their close similarity to many of the disputes and
divisions we face today. Eventually I abandoned the chronological narrative for an ordering based on the issues that
have recurred most often and most prominently in contests
over party reform throughout our history. The latter
ordering was used in the lectures and is continued in the
book.

For their gracious hospitality to my wife and me during
two delightful weeks in Berkeley and the San Francisco
Bay Area I wish to thank the Jefferson Memorial Lectures
Committee, Dean Sanford S. Elberg, Mrs. Ella L. Spon-
seller, and our friends and colleagues Cleo and Heinz
Eulau, Mitzi and Herbert McClosky, Linda and Nelson
Polsby, Lee and Allan Sindler, Ellen and Philip Siegelman,
Brocha and Percy Tannenbaum, Aaron Wildavsky, and
Barbara and Raymond Wolfinger. I also wish to thank
Karen and William McClung for their editorial advice and
encouragement as well as their hospitality.

Finally there is the always impossible task of thanking
adequately those colleagues whose comments and sugges-
tions have given the book much of whatever merit it may
have. Nelson Polsby took much of the sting out of topping
me as Managing Editor of the *American Political Science
Review* by suggesting the topic and encouraging me to
pursue it. As on previous occasions, I shamelessly exploited
the generosity and acumen of Leon Epstein, Anthony
King, Evron Kirkpatrick, Herbert McClosky, and Raymond Wolfinger by asking them to read and comment on

the manuscript. And Joseph A. Ranney III, our family's leading scholar of American history, read the entire manuscript and saved me from many a gaffe of the sort that makes historians despair of political scientists. Whatever pleasure he may get from his part in the dedication can be only a tiny fraction of the pleasure he has given.

I cannot blame any of my mentors for the book's errors. But I hope they will find their efforts not entirely wasted.

A.R.

Madison, Wisconsin
June 1, 1974

CHAPTER ONE

Party Reform in Academic Theory and Political Practice

This book is about the theory and practice of party reform in America. It deals with ideas and events as remote in time as the creation of the world's first modern political party in the 1790s and as recent as this morning's headlines. For, make no mistake about it, we are today right in the midst of one of the greatest waves of party reform in the nation's history.

Consider what has happened in the brief span between 1968 and 1974. The 1968 Democratic national convention ordered the national committee to establish a special commission to draw up rules that would "assure even broader citizen participation in the delegate selection process" and guarantee to all Democratic voters a "full and timely opportunity" to take part. In 1969 the McGovern-Fraser commission[1] carried out this mandate by laying down eighteen guidelines requiring radical changes in the procedures by which the state parties selected their

[1] Its official title was the "Commission on Party Structure and Delegate Selection," but it is generally known by the names of its two chairmen, Senator George S. McGovern of South Dakota (1969-1971) and Representative Donald M. Fraser of Minnesota (1971-1972).

1

delegates to national conventions. In 1971 the Democratic National Committee incorporated all eighteen in its official call for the 1972 convention, and made compliance a precondition for the seating of each state's delegates. Despite this unprecedented national invasion of their historic right to make their own rules, all the state parties got into line. The result was a 1972 convention with far more women, blacks, and young people—and far fewer party notables—than any in history.

The convention made some radical changes of its own. It voted that in 1976 no delegation will be seated *en bloc* if its members have been selected either by a winner-take-all primary, as in California, or by an "open" primary allowing non-Democrats to participate, as in Wisconsin. The convention also abolished the principle of equal state representation which had governed the apportionment of members of the national committee since its establishment in 1848, and adopted a new rule reflecting more accurately the states' numbers of Democratic voters. And it wound up a busy week by ordering a national "Conference on Democratic Party Organization and Policy" to be held in 1974 to decide whether the party should adopt a whole new form of organization. The result just could be a national party reformed out of all recognition.

During these years the Republicans have been the party in control of the Presidency, with no 1968 convention debacle or 1972 election disaster to spur them on. They could not be expected to match the Democrats' hot pace in reform, and they have not. But neither have they been idle. Their 1968 convention directed the national committee to develop ways of implementing the party's Rule 32 providing that participation in party affairs "shall in no way be abridged for reasons of race, religion, color, or national origin." In 1969 the national chairman appointed a Committee on Delegates and Organization (immediately dubbed "the DO Committee"), which recommended ten new rules, most seeking the same goals as the McGovern-Fraser guidelines. The 1972 convention adopted nearly all of them, and ordered them made effective for selecting delegates to the 1976 convention.

Taken together then, the two national parties have made more reforms from 1968 to 1974 than at any time since the death of the congressional caucus and the birth of the national conventions in the 1820s and 1830s. Even so, reforms recently made or contemplated by the national and state governments may yet overshadow what the parties have done. For example, between 1969 and 1973 no fewer than eight states newly adopted presidential primaries. This was by far the most added in any comparable period since the primaries first operated in 1912, and the resulting total of twenty-four was the highest in history. In 1968 less than half of the delegates to either convention were elected or bound by primaries; in 1972 it was two-thirds, and in 1976 it will be nearly 70 percent. Moreover, Congress is now considering more seriously than ever before legislation to establish a national primary. To top it off, after nearly two centuries of treating the national parties and their procedures as purely private affairs, some federal courts are now declaring that national party processes are integral parts of the presidential selection process and are therefore subject to judicial review in all their aspects. The Supreme Court has not yet ruled on this issue, but it soon will.

Thus any contemporary book on party reform deals with one of America's most lively areas of political ferment and change. This particular book is rooted in two of its author's main involvements. The first is my longstanding professional concern with why American political parties behave as they do and with the proposals, made mostly by academic political scientists for "responsible party government"—that is, a government like Great Britain's in which all policy is made by a cohesive, and therefore responsible, governing party. The second is my reflections upon my experiences from 1969 to 1972 as one of the two professorial members of the McGovern-Fraser commission. Both involvements will manifest themselves many times over in the chapters to come.

At the outset, however, the reader is entitled to ask about the topic of this (or any) book: Who cares? What does it matter? The answer to the first question is that some political scientists and a good many politicians demonstrably care. The answer to the second is less obvious, but many who have been involved in party reform would agree with me that it matters considerably for the quality of American political life. Yet the latter proposition needs a case made for it, not merely an assertion; and making it is one of the main tasks of this introductory chapter.

In logic, if not in historic experience, two questions precede all others in considering party reform. The first asks to what degree the peculiar characteristics of America's political parties are an important cause or a visible effect of their constitutional and socioeconomic environment. The second asks whether it is even possible, let alone desirable, to change the environment by changing the parties. Let us begin by reviewing what has been said about both questions by the scholars most concerned.

THE PRIMACY AND MALLEABILITY OF PARTIES

If one measures the scholarly impact of a book by how many academics have felt compelled to respond to it, then surely E.E. Schattschneider's *Party Government*, published in 1942, is one of the most seminal works of twentieth century political science.[2] Not least of the reasons for its impact was its vigorous and, to some, persuasive argument

[2] *Party Government* (New York: Farrar and Rinehart, 1942). The

4

that political parties play a crucial role in modern democratic government. Schattschneider began with this often quoted pronouncement:

> The rise of political parties is indubitably one of the principal distinguishing marks of modern government. The parties, in fact, have played a major role as *makers* of governments, more especially they have been the makers of democratic government. It should be stated flatly at the outset that this volume is devoted to the thesis that the political parties created democracy and that modern democracy is unthinkable save in terms of the parties. . . . The parties are not therefore merely appendages of modern government; they are in the center of it and play a determinative and creative role in it.[3]

This same belief in the primacy of parties was held by Woodrow Wilson, Henry Jones Ford, Frank J. Goodnow, and the other turn-of-the-century political scientists who first developed the doctrine of responsible party government.[4] It has also been assumed or proclaimed by the writers who have expounded the responsible-parties view in our own time.[5] After Schattschneider's, its most impres-

---

most comprehensive critique of the literature supporting, amending, and attacking Schattschneider's position is Evron M. Kirkpatrick, "Toward a More Responsible Two-Party System: Political Science, Policy Science, or Pseudo-Science?," *American Political Science Review*, 65 (December, 1971) 965-990.

[3] *Party Government*, p. 1, emphasis in the original.

[4] Their views and relevance for current discussions of parties are described in my *The Doctrine of Responsible Party Government* (Urbana, Ill.: University of Illinois Press, 1954, 1962).

[5] The leading advocates include: Stephen K. Bailey, *The Condition of Our National Political Parties* (New York: Fund for the Republic, 1959); James MacGregor Burns, *The Deadlock of Democracy* (Englewood Cliffs, N.J.: Prentice-Hall, 1963); and David S. Broder, *The Party's Over: The Failure of Politics in America* (New York: Harper & Row, 1972). An interesting variation is Judson L. James' advocacy

sive statement was this declaration made in 1950 by the Committee on Political Parties of the American Political Science Association (which Schattschneider chaired):

> Throughout this report political parties are treated as indispensable instruments of government. That is to say, we proceed on the proposition that *popular government in a nation of more than 150 million people requires political parties which provide the electorate with a proper range of choice between alternatives of action.* The party system thus serves as the main device for bringing into continuing relationship those ideas about liberty, majority rule and leadership which Americans are largely taking for granted.[6]

The advocates of responsible party government have argued not only that parties are primary but also that they are malleable. They agree with William Nisbet Chambers that

> modern parties and the party system in the United States were indeed products of a labor of Hercules, and not "natural," unintended flowerings from the soil of independence and popular government. Rather, parties were ingeniously shaped "artifacts," in the sense of structures built up over the years by the industrious, if often groping, activities of men.[7]

---

of more responsible parties coupled with opposition to responsible party government of the Schattschneider variety: *American Political Parties: Potential and Performance* (New York: Western, 1969).

[6] "Toward a More Responsible Two-Party System; a Report of the Committee on Political Parties, American Political Science Association," *American Political Science Review*, 44 (September, 1950, supplement), p. 15, emphasis in the original.

[7] William Nisbet Chambers, *Political Parties in a New Nation* (New York: Oxford University Press, 1963), p. 10.

Party Reform in Theory and Practice

If the parties have indeed been made by the conscious, purposive efforts of people, then it follows that they can be reformed whenever the people have the will to reform them. Schattschneider, for example, rejected the often heard argument that the parties' decentralization and low cohesion are the inescapable consequences of constitutional federalism and separation of powers. Parties, he said, have a way of bending these legal structures to their own extralegal purposes: look at how they got around the electoral college system by making presidential nominations and pledging electors to vote for them. What, then, is needed now to make the parties cohesive and responsible? First and foremost, he replied, is to develop the necessary popular will:

> The greatest difficulties in the way of the development of party government in the United States have been intellectual, not legal. It is not unreasonable to suppose that once a respectable section of the public understands the issue, ways of promoting party government through the Constitution can be found.[8]

The doctrine of responsible party government has not lacked academic critics, either in Wilson's time or Schattschneider's. Some have agreed that parties are indeed key institutions and responsible parties are the best kind, but have disputed the contention that American parties are irresponsible.[9] Others have also accepted the primacy of parties but have argued that British-style disciplined and centralized parties are so contrary to the values of most Americans that they are not likely to be

[8] *Party Government,* pp. 209-210.
[9] This is the essential argument of Julius Turner, "Responsible Parties: A Dissent from the Floor," *American Political Science Review,* 45 (March, 1951), 143-152.

embraced here and would not be desirable if they were.[10]

In recent years, however, several political scientists have strongly challenged *both* the primacy and malleability notions—and perhaps also, at least by implication, the premise of this book: that party reform makes a major difference. For instance, Anthony King notes that most college textbooks on parties list a number of functions parties are said to perform in modern Western democracies—for example, structuring the vote, organizing government, and aggregating interests. He surveys how these functions are actually performed in Western societies, including the United States, and finds that parties play only secondary roles in their performance. He concludes:

> on the basis of the discussion it would seem that we are entitled, at the very least, to a certain scepticism concerning the standard catalog of party functions, and also concerning the great importance attached to parties in large segments of the political science literature.[11]

Similarly, Leon D. Epstein and Frank J. Sorauf call attention to the parties' declining part in such traditional

[10] This argument was first made by A. Lawrence Lowell in *Essays on Government* (Boston: Houghton Mifflin, 1897), esp. pp. 21-22, 90-108. It has since been made by, among others, T. William Goodman, "How Much Political Party Centralization Do We Want?", *Journal of Politics*, 13 (November, 1951), 536-561; Murray S. Stedman, Jr. and Herbert Sonthoff, "Party Responsibilty—A Critical Inquiry," *Western Political Quarterly*, 4 (September, 1951), 454-468; and my "Toward a More Responsible Two-Party System: A Commentary," *American Political Science Review*, 45 (June 1951), 488-499.

[11] Anthony King, "Political Parties in Western Democracies: Some Sceptical Reflections," *Polity*, 1 (Winter 1969), 140. Similar, though not identical, conclusions are reached in Howard A. Scarrow, "The Function of Political Parties: A Critique of the Literature and the Approach," *Journal of Politics*, 29 (November 1967), 770-790; and Theodore J. Lowi, "Toward Functionalism in Political Science: The Case of Innovation in Party Systems," *American Political Science Review*, 57 (September 1963), 570-583.

activities as recruiting political leaders and organizing and financing campaigns. Both emphasize the growing importance in these matters of nonparty movements and candidate-centered organizations. Epstein concludes that "parties can be viewed as important but not overwhelmingly important political agencies" and asks "why should [parties] be thought so important that their effectiveness determines the effectiveness of the [whole political] system?"[12]

Furthermore, Epstein and Sorauf agree with William J. Keefe's judgment that American parties are more the offspring of their environment than the progenitors of its special characteristics. The words which begin Keefe's book stand in sharp contrast to those which begin Schattschneider's:

Any attempt to unravel the mysteries of American political parties might well begin with the recognition of this fact: The parties are less what they make of themselves than what their environment makes of them. The parties are not free to develop in any fashion that they might like, to take on any organizational form that might appear desirable, to pursue any course of action that might seem to be required, or to assume any responsibility that might appear appropriate. The truth of the matter is that the shape of American parties is strongly influenced by the design of the legal-political system, the election system, the political culture, and the heterogeneous quality of American life. To a remarkable extent, the party system owes its form and substance to the impact of external elements.[13]

[12] Leon D. Epstein, *Political Parties in Western Democracies* (New York: Frederick A. Praeger, 1967), p. 8, and also Chs. I and IX; see also Frank J. Sorauf, *Party Politics in America* (2nd ed., Boston: Little, Brown, 1972), pp. 415-419, 432.

[13] William J. Keefe, *Parties, Politics, and Public Policy in America*

Curing the Mischiefs of Faction

In Keefe's view, significant changes in the structure and behavior of parties will come, if at all, only slowly as the result of prior changes in their controlling environment. In much the same mood, Sorauf concluded in 1964—five years before the McGovern-Fraser commission announced its new rules—that:

> The years of the 1950's and 1960's have been years of affluence and satisfaction in American politics. Any number of commentators have spoken of the disinterest, the deadlock, the immobilism of the politics of the postwar years. . . . In such a period of drift and stalemate few political issues are resolved. Certainly it is not the time for a dramatic testing of party machinery or for demands for reform and change.[14]

Thus our most eminent scholars of parties cannot agree upon either the primacy or the malleability of these peculiar institutions. But they are not the only people who think the questions are important. As we shall detail in this book, from the 1790s to the 1970s thousands of Americans have been absorbed in struggles over hundreds of proposals for party reform. However they may have felt about particular proposals, they have all agreed, tacitly or explicitly, on at least these four propositions: First, the structure of a party's organization, whatever may be its ultimate significance or insignificance for the Republic, has a profound influence on contests to win the party's nominations, elect its candidates, distribute its patronage, formulate its programs, and allocate whatever other goods its members seek. Second, the party's structure is deter-

(New York: Holt, Rinehart and Winston, 1972), p. 1. For Epstein's similar view, see Epstein *op, cit.*, pp. 8-9.

[14] Frank J. Sorauf, *Political Parties in the American System* (Boston: Little, Brown, 1964), p. 57.

mined most immediately by the content, interpretation, and application of its own rules and the relevant public laws. Third, people can and do preserve or change the party's structure by making and amending the rules and laws. And fourth, the contests between those who urge and those who resist particular reform proposals are real fights over important stakes, and any party politician who recognizes that such a fight may put his own position in the balance has no choice but to participate.

Thus party politicians generally view the primacy of party reform and the malleability of party rules quite differently than do many academics. Take, for example, the McGovern-Fraser commission's reforms. Political scientists should and do raise the question of whether the reforms made or accelerated any changes of major and enduring significance for the American political system.[15] That is a proper job for political scientists. But few Democratic politicians doubt that the reforms radically altered the party's ways of selecting its national convention delegates, or that the changes drastically changed the power positions of, among others, George McGovern, Richard Daley, Jesse Jackson, and George Wallace, or that the reforms produced a 1972 national convention very different from any in history, or that the convention's new character profoundly affected the party's moral title to popular support and its practical ability to win it (the two are not quite the same thing). As I write, Democratic activists of several different persuasions are preparing for the next rounds of the reform battle to be fought in 1974 and beyond. Most do not question that the battle must be fought or that it makes a real difference who wins.

The Democrats' clash over the McGovern-Fraser reforms is only one of the most recent of many in American

[15] For one such assessment, see Bill Cavala, "Changing the Rules Changes the Game," *American Political Science Review* (March, 1974).

history. The purpose of this book is to describe the main ideas and interests competing in the major disputes and to analyze the causes and consequences of their outcomes. As noted in the Preface, I originally intended to proceed by chronological order. However, the more I learned about the earlier reform fights the more I was impressed by how similar were many of the arguments made and the interests involved to those I had observed during my participation in the McGovern-Fraser reform disputes. I therefore decided to focus on what I have come to see as the most fundamental and recurring *issues* of party reform. Each of the chapters to follow will deal with a different set of these issues.

This decision has one cost I hope to minimize here. Some readers may, like me, not be specialists in American political history and thus may not be familiar with all of the events considered in later chapters. Accordingly, I shall conclude this introduction by presenting a brief, but I hope useful, narrative of the chief episodes which provide most of the book's material.

PARTY REFORM IN AMERICAN HISTORY

Throughout the book I use the term "party reform" to denote the adoption of party rules and public laws intended to alter the structure and behavior of an established party or party system.[16] In this formulation party reform can be said to take place, strictly speaking, only after an organized party system has been established in

[16] There is a considerable dispute among political scientists about the proper definitions of "party" and "party system." It seems excessive to explore the matter here, but for a review of the main positions taken and my own efforts to synthesize them, see "The Concept of 'Party,'" in Oliver Garceau (ed.), *Political Research and Political Theory* (Cambridge, Mass.: Harvard University Press, 1968), pp. 143-162.

all essentials and only when it is perceived to have affected political life sufficiently to be worth reforming.

Most historians agree that the United States is the first nation in which this became the case. The process began in the early 1790s and was substantially complete by 1820. And, as we shall note in a moment, it was followed in the early 1820s by the first of our three main epochs of party reform.

American political parties grew, so to speak, from the inside out. They began in the early 1790s with the assembling of regular private meetings, or "caucuses," of "republican" congressmen to pool their resources and plan their tactics to block Alexander Hamilton's policies. The Hamiltonians, or "federalists," had no choice but to defend their program by counter-organization. Thus by 1800 both parties had developed extensive intragovernmental organizations centered on their congressional caucuses. And in 1800 each caucus moved into presidential politics by choosing the party's candidate and pledging its adherents in the electoral college to vote for him. The Republicans kept up the practice until the 1820s, but the Federalists experimented with several other methods after 1800 in an effort to recoup their steadily sagging electoral fortunes.

Both parties soon learned that purely intragovernmental organization was not enough. To win its objectives each needed not only unity among its elected officials but also enough of them to outvote the opposition. So in the early 1790s first the Republicans and then the Federalists began to encourage the formation of extragovernmental party organizations in various localities for the purpose of choosing and supporting party candidates for the House of Representatives. These state and local caucuses and committees soon added efforts to elect governors, state legislators, and other state and local officials. Thus by the early

1800s the two parties largely monopolized the nominations of and campaigns for most candidates for most elective offices at all levels.

Until well into the nineteenth century most nominations for local offices were made by informal mass meetings of the local party adherents, generally called "caucuses" or "primaries." In the 1790s nominations for statewide offices were generally made by caucuses in the state capital, but by the early 1800s this had come to seem so unfair to party members in the rest of the state that the nominating function was taken over by the party's caucus in the state legislature. In some states these "legislative caucuses" became "mixed caucuses" by being augmented with delegates elected by party meetings in districts in which the party had no elected legislator. And in a few states the mixed caucuses were supplanted by state conventions composed entirely of delegates elected by the local party meetings.

In the 1790s the two original parties were almost even in strength, with the Federalists having a slight edge at the national level. However, the smashing triumph of Jefferson and his Republicans in the watershed election of 1800 dealt the Federalists a blow from which they never recovered. Thereafter their numbers steadily dwindled in Congress and in most state and local governments. All their presidential nominees lost, and after the crushing defeat of Rufus King in 1816 they nominated no more. Soon thereafter their organization, if not their ideas, disappeared altogether.

Thus by 1820 there was only one American party, but that party possessed an elaborate set of national, state, and local organs and rules. Being thus established, those organs and rules became potential targets for reform; and that potential was soon realized in the first of America's three main epochs of party reform.

Party Reform in Theory and Practice

The first major drive for party reform was the effort in the early 1820s to end presidential nominations by the Republicans' congressional caucus, a practice that had been followed consistently from 1800 to 1816 (none was held in 1820 because of the certainty of Monroe's renomination). In later chapters we shall examine the doctrines and the factional and candidate interests involved in the fight over this proposed reform and shall weigh the outcome's consequences. For the present it is enough to note that, while the proreform forces persuaded a number of state legislatures and local mass meetings to denounce "King Caucus," their main efforts were concentrated on persuading Republican congressmen to boycott the caucus called for 1824. They succeeded: only 66 of the party's 216 members attended the caucus, and the candidate they nominated, William H. Crawford, eventually received only 41 of the 261 electoral votes. Never since has a party's congressional caucus nominated a presidential condidate; and whatever chances the nation might have had to develop a form of parliamentary or cabinet government was gone forever. Thus the first effort at party reform won a total and permanent victory, one with major consequences for the evolution of the political system.

For the next few years the Republicans remained the only national party, but their various factions soon began to coalesce into two opposing groups: Andrew Jackson's "Democratic Republicans" and Henry Clay's "National Republicans." Presidential nominations by congressional caucus were replaced in the late 1820s by a series of state-based devices, principally nominations by state legislatures and by state legislative caucuses. These sufficed to put forth Jackson and the incumbent John Quincy Adams as the two nominees in 1828, and Jackson won the election handily. The National Republicans soon thereafter became an entirely separate party. One of their first decisions was the conclusion that Jackson's popularity forced them to abandon state-based nominations and set up a truly national nominating procedure to concert all the nation's anti-Jackson forces behind one national candidate. They chose for this purpose the device pioneered by the minor Anti-Masonic Party in 1830, and in 1831 the National Republicans brought off history's second great party reform by holding a national nominating convention in Baltimore which nominated Henry Clay to oppose Jackson. The Democratic Republicans had no question about the identity of their presidential nominee for 1832, but the Jackson forces resolved to drop John C. Calhoun as the vice-presidential candidate and to replace him with Martin Van Buren. Given Calhoun's many friends in Congress, the best strategy seemed to be to call their own national convention outside Washington which they assembled in Baltimore in 1832. Since then all major party presidential and vice-presidential candidates have been nominated by national delegate conventions.

It is worth noting that most of the procedures adopted for the first conventions of 1831 and 1832 continued unchanged until well into the twentieth century. For instance, the basis for apportioning delegates among the state parties was the states' votes in the electoral college rather than their populations or party voting strengths. That remained the rule for both parties until the Republicans pioneered the "bonus vote" principle in 1916. Again, while the early national conventions themselves decided how many votes and delegates each state should have, they left it entirely to the states and state parties to decide *how* their allotted delegates would be selected. That remained the case until the 1960s. In addition, in 1832 the Democrats adopted a rule requiring a two-thirds majority for winning their nominations, a rule that survived until 1936. The Democrats also adopted the "unit rule," which allowed a state party to insist that its delegation's entire vote be cast and counted as the delegation's majority directed; that rule lasted until 1968.

After 1832 many changes took place in the party system, but only a few in the parties' internal organizations. By 1840 regular two-party competition was restored in the "second party system" alignment of Democrats against Whigs (*née* National Republicans). The second system survived for two decades but collapsed in the 1850s under the terrible pressures of the slavery and secession issues. After a period of confusion and realignment lasting until the late 1860s, the "third party system" aligning Democrats against Republicans (the new party with the old name) was established by 1868 and has persisted to today. But from the 1840s until well after the Civil War there was little agitation for intraparty reform. In 1848 the Democrats established a national committee to preside over national party affairs between conventions, and the new Republicans did the same in 1854. In 1866 both parties' congressional wings established congressional campaign committees, thereby widening the breach opened in 1824 between the "congressional" and "presidential" parties. But neither of these changes stirred much conflict or attracted much attention.

THE PROGRESSIVE REFORMS, 1890-1920

In the two decades after Appomattox the parties moved nearer the center of public attention than ever before. No longer were they generally regarded as accidental parasites that could be removed at will. Most politicians and voters, and even a few daring political scientists, concluded that the parties were here to stay. Many, indeed, regarded them as the prime shapers of the political system and therefore the causes of the corruption and unresponsiveness of government which some felt were dragging the nation down from the 1870s on. One of the results of this attitude was that for the first time in history party reform was widely held to be not merely important but the indispensable first step toward all other political and social reform.

This belief was a prime article of faith in what historians have named the "progressive movement." Led from the nid-1880s to the early 1920s by some of the most adroit and inspired politicians in our history, most notably Robert M. La Follette, the progressives carried through the second, and in some respects the most extensive, wave of party reform.

The main progressive reforms will be discussed at length in later chapters, but they should be listed briefly here. The first was the adoption by most states from 1890 to 1920 of elaborate legal codes closely regulating the state parties' internal affairs: the codes generally stipulated what committees and conventions the parties must have, the procedures by which their members are selected, who may participate in making the parties' decisions, and what powers, if any, each party organ has over the others. The second was the establishment in many municipalities from the early 1900s on of legally nonpartisan elections, whereby the party affiliations of candidates for public office are not listed on the official ballots. And the third was the most radical of all the progressive reforms, indeed the most radical party reform yet adopted: the nearly universal legal imposition after 1904 of the direct primary

The progressive reforms thus not only created most of the legal environment in which our state parties still live; they profoundly affected the national parties as well. Many analysts here and abroad, from Lord Bryce and A.

Lawrence Lowell in the nineteenth century to Maurice Duverger and Leon D. Epstein in the twentieth, have noted how different America's major parties are from their counterparts in other Western democracies. And few would dispute that the progressive reforms contributed more than those of any other epoch to making our parties what they are today. But even the La Follette era did not end the story of party reform.

THE MODERN REFORMS, 1952-?

We noted at the outset that Americans are now living in the midst of the nation's third great epoch of party reform. Most of the action has taken place since 1952 in the national parties, and it has had two main thrusts. The first has been the claim established by the national committees and conventions of both parties that they and not their state and local affiliates have the ultimate control over the membership of the national agencies. The second and more widely discussed thrust has been the efforts of both parties to make their procedures for selecting national convention delegates more open and the conventions more representative.

I have already outlined the main events from 1968 to 1973. Those prior to 1968 can be briefly told. In 1952 the Democratic national committeeman from Texas openly supported the Republican presidential candidate: Soon thereafter the national committee refused to seat him and rejected the Texas party's claim that the DNC had to accept anyone certified by a state party. After going without a committeeman for three years the Texas party finally capitulated, naming an acceptable substitute in 1955. In 1958 the Louisiana Democratic party tried to remove its national committeeman for being "soft" on questions of racial segregation. The DNC insisted on its right to be the sole judge of its members' qualifications. They rejected the Louisiana party's action, refused to accept any successor, and continued to treat the incumbent as the state's legitimate representative.

In 1956 the Democratic national convention adopted a rule that each state party must, as a condition for having its delegates seated, ensure that the party's national nominees will appear on the state's ballot as the regular Democratic nominees. In 1964 the convention added the rule that a state party must guarantee that there is no racial discrimination preventing full participation in its affairs; and in 1968 the entire Mississippi delegation and half the Georgia delegation were denied seats because their parties were found to have violated this rule.

The most radical reforms have been made since 1968, as we have seen. Being in the midst of this third major epoch of party reform, we can only speculate about its final shape, extent, and consequences. But there is no gainsaying the fact that, whatever political scientists may think about the primacy and malleability of parties, many political activists in our own time, just like those of Jackson's time and La Follette's, do not doubt that the parties' rules and structures can be changed and that changing them has important consequences for both the participants and the polity.

The extensive changes made in the historic course of American party reform add up to a volume of reform far greater than that in any other Western nation. Our central concern in the chapters to follow will be the consequences of those reforms for the nature of our parties and the quality of our political life. But first it seems important to ask *why* Americans have reworked their parties so often and so extensively. A good deal of the answer, I believe, lies in the fact that party reform has always seemed to many a welcome escape from dilemmas arising from the fundamental ambivalence that has always characterized the attitudes of most Americans toward political parties and political action. That ambivalence is the topic of the next chapter.

CHAPTER TWO

American Ambivalence About Political Parties

An epigraph for this book might well have been taken from the late Dag Hammarskjöld, who knew only too well the gap between the lofty ideas of humanity and the actual behavior of people. "The road to holiness," he observed, "necessarily passes through the world of action."[1]

His observation is fitting because in the long and convoluted epic that is the story of party reform in America, one leitmotiv appears more often than any other. This is the tendency of Americans to deal uneasily with the necessities of partisan political organization because of their widespread belief that political parties are, at best, unavoidable evils whose propensities for divisiveness, oligarchy, and corruption must be closely watched and sternly controlled.

The persistence of this combination of antiparty thought and partisan action throughout our history has been noted by several writers, particularly Noble E. Cunningham, Jr., Richard Hofstadter, Allan P. Sindler, and Frank J. Sorauf.[2] It can be illustrated with examples from

[1] *Markings*, translated from the Swedish by Leif Sjöber and W.H. Auden, (New York: Alfred A. Knopf, 1964), p. 122.

[2] See Noble E. Cunningham, Jr. (ed.), *The Making of the American Party System, 1789 to 1809* (Englewood Cliffs, N.J.: Prentice-Hall,

22

each of the three main epochs of party reform outlined in Chapter 1. The earliest is provided by James Madison, who was not only the nation's first seminal theorist of the institution of parties but also its first great party organizer. In early 1788 Madison published the Tenth Federalist paper, which set forth a view of political organization that has dominated much American thinking ever since. He began by declaring that the greatest danger to the American union, as to all republican governments, is "their propensity to [the] dangerous vice of faction." Human beings, he observed, differ from one another in many ways: some are rich, some poor; some are merchants, some farmers; some are Protestants, some Catholics; and so on. Their different characteristics, in turn, generate different interests. Consequently, what favors one group disadvantages another, and what government does to help one is bound to harm another.

This fact of social life, Madison continued, is the basic source of "faction" and "party" in a free society. He used the two terms interchangeably to denote organizations created to promote particular interests against their competitors. Each organization strives to concert its resources to induce government to adopt some policies and reject others. Thus conflict among parties/factions is inevitable. Left unrestrained, it will surely tear the nation asunder until it is ended by the victory of one party/faction over all the others.

Therefore, Madison warned, the first objective of any republican government must be the search for "methods of curing the mischiefs of faction." That search can move

---

1965), pp. 1, 65-74; Richard Hofstadter, *The Idea of a Party System* (Berkeley, Los Angeles and London: University of California Press, 1970), pp. ix, 1; Allan P. Sindler, *Political Parties in the United States* (New York: St. Martin's Press, 1966), p. 5; and Frank J. Sorauf, "Extra-Legal Political Parties in Wisconsin," *American Political Science Review*, 48 (September, 1954), 692.

in either of two directions: "the one, by removing its causes; the other, by controlling its effects."[3] But the causes can be removed only by severely abridging the citizens' freedom of speech and assembly, and that is too great a price to pay for even so noble an object. Consequently, those who cherish freedom must seek to cure the mischiefs of faction by controlling its effects. And their basic strategy, in Madison's view, must be to divide the power of government into many parcels and to distribute them among the national and state levels of government and, at each level, among the legislative, executive, and judicial branches. Such a fragmentation and dispersion of power, he believed, will make it impossible for a single party/faction to seize all power and impose its will everywhere. Only in this way can the republic cure the mischiefs of faction without sacrificing freedom.

So said James Madison the political theorist in 1788. But less than two years later James Madison the politician joined Thomas Jefferson in a resolute effort to resist the foreign and domestic policies of Alexander Hamilton. Neither Madison nor Jefferson abandoned their philosophical view that parties are divisive and dangerous.[4] But, like anyone who acts in as well as writes about politics, they were faced with a fact, not a theory. The fact was that Hamilton's designs could be defeated only by unifying the anti-Hamiltonians in Congress and by increasing their number in the elections of 1792 and after. So the two Virginians took their famous "botanizing" tour of the northern states in May, 1791, and put together the Republican party. And so it was that James Madison,

---

[3] Roy F. Fairfield (ed.), *The Federalist Papers* (New York: Anchor Books, 1961), p. 17. Other references to the Tenth Paper are from this edition.

[4] Hofstadter shows convincingly that Jefferson's attitudes toward parties, while neither so systematic nor so well developed as Madison's, were substantially the same: Hofstadter, *op. cit.*, pp. 151, 204-205.

the distinguished antiparty political theorist, became the cofounder of the world's first modern political party.[5]

A century later, Robert Marion La Follette of Madison, Wisconsin combined eloquent antiorganization rhetoric with skilled factional infighting to win control of an established party. In 1896 and again in 1898 he sought the Republican nomination for governor in the party's state convention, but both times was passed over for a more conservative candidate. After he finally won the nomination and the office in 1900, he resolved to end the conservatives' "boss rule" which had beaten him before and might beat him again. The only hope for true democracy, he argued, was to take the nominating power away from the bosses and restore it to the people by means of the direct primary; for democracy dies when any self-selected organization is allowed to intrude itself between the sovereign people and their free choice of public officials. A typical trumpet blast came in his first speech to the legislature in 1901:

> It is the essence of republican government that the citizen should act for himself directly wherever possible. In the exercise of no other right is this so important as in the nomination of candidates for office. . . . If between the citizen and the official there is a complicated system of caucuses and conventions, by the easy manipulations of which the selection of

[5] For a detailed account of Madison's movement from antiparty theorist to party organizer, see Irving Brant, *James Madison: Father of the Constitution, 1787-1800* (Indianapolis, Ind.: Bobbs-Merrill, 1950), esp. Chs. 23 and 27. For accounts of similar combinations of antiparty thought and partisan action in other political leaders of the 1790s and early 1800s, see Cunningham, *op. cit.*; William Nisbet Chambers, *Political Parties in a New Nation* (New York: Oxford University Press, 1963); and Joseph Charles, *The Origins of the American Party System* (Williamsburg, Va.: Institute of Early American History and Culture, 1956).

candidates is controlled by some other agency or power, then the official will so render his services as to have the approval of such an agency or power. The overwhelming demand of the people of this state. . .is that such intervening power and authority, and the complicated system which sustains it, shall be torn down and cast aside.[6]

The legislature, however, defeated La Follette's primary bill in 1901. He immediately set to work putting together a "reform machine." He dexterously used patronage appointments, stump oratory, legislative logrolling, and any other method that seemed useful to convert or defeat his political opponents. As one of his leading biographers concludes, "In every essential La Follette was a 'reform boss.'"[7]

His machine to end machines worked magnificently, and in 1903 a purified and chastened legislature adopted the nation's first general and mandatory direct primary law. But, like so many other famous victories, it soon turned sour. In the first primary election held under the new law the people of Wisconsin showed their ingratitude by rejecting a number of the La Follette faction's candidates. Particularly galling was the primary defeat in 1908 of La Follette's chief legislative lieutenant, Herman Ekern. One might have expected the Progressives' principles to make them accept the primary's verdict as the will of the people, but not so. Ekern ran as an independent in the

[6] Message to the legislature, 1901, in Ellen Torelle (ed.), *The Political Philosophy of Robert M. La Follette as Revealed in His Speeches and Writings* (Madison, Wis.: Robert M. La Follette Co., 1920), pp. 39-40.

[7] Robert S. Maxwell, *La Follette and the Rise of the Progressives in Wisconsin* (Madison, Wis.: State Historical Society, 1956), p. 58; for accounts of the La Follette "machine's" techniques and success, see pp. 56-64. See Richard Hofstadter, *The Age of Reform* (New York: Vintage Books, 1955), pp. 7, 269-270.

general election, and La Follette stumped the district for him. Once more, however, the district's sovereign people rejected this interference with their right to choose, and defeated Ekern again.[8] In the next few years the Progressives lost so many primaries that they decided to hold preprimary conventions to improve their chances. La Follette could not bring himself to endorse publicly so flagrant a repudiation of Progressive principles, but he was not unhappy with its contribution to his faction's cause.[9]

The most successful movement for party reform in our own time has worthily continued this venerable American combination of antipartisan principle with partisan activity. In subsequent chapters we shall examine some of the forces that from 1968 to 1972 changed many of the Democratic party's structures and procedures and won the presidential nomination for George McGovern. For present purposes we need only note that one of the main commitments of the McGovern reformers was to the principle that all participants in the party's affairs, from local caucuses to the national convention, should speak and vote according to their own consciences, not in submission to the orders of any party notable or "boss." Thus the report of the McGovern-Fraser reform commission observed that past national convention delegates had been "frequently required to cast votes against their personal preferences—indeed against their consciences."[10] To end all that the commission adopted new rules which, among other things, abolished proxy voting and the unit rule, ended

[8] See Herbert F. Margulies, *The Decline of the Progressive Movement in Wisconsin, 1890-1920* (Madison, Wis.: State Historical Society, 1962), pp. 83-103, 121, 151.

[9] Descriptions of the Progressive faction's efforts to organize preprimary conventions and La Follette's reactions to them are given in *ibid.*, pp. 122, 283-284.

[10] Commission on Party Structure and Delegate Selection, *Mandate for Reform* (Washington, D.C.: Democratic National Committee, 1970), p. 22.

"favorite son" delegations, prohibited ex officio delegates, and called for the fair representation of minority views on presidential candidates and, presumably, on platform planks as well.[11] The O'Hara Commission on Convention Rules went one step further by stipulating that the "Chairman of the Convention shall not be allowed to enforce any provision of State law, party rule, resolution or instruction which shall purport to instruct any delegate how to cast his vote. . . . What may prompt a delegate to vote as he does is a matter between the delegate and his conscience or his constituency."[12]

In the benign climate created by the new rules, McGovern's army of dedicated issue-oriented activists won control of the convention and the nomination for their leader. They also caused him some problems. Many McGovernites favored some highly controversial proposals for the platform—notably one for a guaranteed annual income of $6500 for each family of four, another for abortion on demand for any woman, another for complete amnesty for all draft evaders, and still another for the repeal of all laws against homosexual relations between consenting adults.

The McGovern organization's strategists were not eager to have these proposals adopted. So, despite whatever qualms they had about interfering with the delegates' consciences and freedom to vote, they distributed mimeographed sheets urging negative votes on the proposals—arguing that if they were adopted they would weaken McGovern's chances of defeating Nixon in November. This plea to sacrifice principle to expedience was very much in the style of the "old" politics and deeply offended those of McGovern's supporters most devoted to the "new." Their disgust was pungently expressed by the Women's Libera-

---

[11] Guidelines B-1, B-5, B-6, and C-2 in *ibid.*, pp. 42-46.

[12] Commission on Rules, *Call to Order* (Washington, D.C.: Democratic National Committee, 1972), p. 58.

tion leader Germaine Greer in a postconvention magazine article entitled "McGovern, the Big Tease." The "McGovern machine," said Ms. Greer, shamelessly sold out the abortion proposal by having "the McGovern whips [instruct] the delegates to avoid the necessity of a roll call by shouting the [proposal] down."[13]

But, in the well-established American tradition, most of the McGovern delegates accepted the necessities of partisan action, set aside their antiorganization principles and policy preferences, and voted as their leader had asked. Ms. Greer was appalled by "the secret dealings, the hypocrisy, the tantalization and the bamboozlement, the coarsening and cheapening of every issue, [and] the abandonment of imagination and commitment for the gray areas of consensus." She was especially disgusted with McGovern's women delegates for succumbing to male chauvinism and the old politics. "Womanlike," she concluded, "they did not want to get tough with their man, and so, womanlike, they got screwed."[14]

The Madison, La Follette, and McGovern episodes illustrate the ambivalence of political leaders and activists about parties and political organization which runs throughout the history of party reform in America. In each of its three main epochs the conflict over reform has been fought mainly over one or more of three tough and persistent questions. First, should the parties be treated as public agencies or private associations? Second, what should the parties do and be prevented from doing? And third, who should control the parties' decisions? Each of the succeeding chapters will focus on one of these questions. In each we shall consider such matters as the forces inside the parties and out which have fought for and against proposed

[13] Germaine Greer, "McGovern, the Big Tease," *Harper's*, 245 (October, 1972), 67.
[14] *Ibid.*, pp. 71, 63.

reforms, what they have stood to gain or lose, and how the parties and the larger political system were changed by the outcomes.

In the remainder of this chapter I shall finish setting the stage by reviewing what America's political leaders and ordinary citizens from Madison's time to McGovern's have thought about parties. This review will, I believe, show that in all eras many Americans have welcomed reform as a handy escape from the dilemma of squaring the necessities of political organization and action with the principled distrust of political parties.

ATTITUDES TOWARD PARTIES: THE LEADERS

From our national beginnings, America's political and intellectual leaders have had a good deal more to say than their counterparts in other lands about the proper role and organization of parties. On this topic they can be classified into one of three main types, which I shall call "the Abolitionists," "the Defenders," and "the Reformers."[15] I shall consider each in turn.

THE ABOLITIONISTS

Richard Hofstadter has shown that in Britain, France, and America in the eighteenth century most right-thinking people regarded political parties and party conflict as evil in intent and disastrous in effect—epidemic diseases of the body politic to be quarantined and stamped out wherever possible.[16] Political theorists and public leaders as various

[15] These categories are comparable in content, though not in labels, to those used by Richard Hofstadter in *The Idea of a Party System*, cited in note 2. Willmoore Kendall and I used similar categories in our earlier *Democracy and the American Party System* (New York: Harcourt, Brace, 1956), Ch. 6.

[16] See Hofstadter, *The Idea of a Party System*, pp. 12-16; and Ranney and Kendall, *op. cit.*, pp. 118-121.

as the Marquis of Halifax, Viscount Bolingbroke, John Trenchard, Thomas Gordon, Jean Jacques Rousseau, Alexander Hamilton, George Washington, and John Taylor of Caroline condemned parties and all their works. The standard indictment included the following main counts.

First, unity, cooperation, and consensus among all citizens is the only basis for promoting the public welfare in the good society. Whatever nurtures patriotic unity is good, and whatever evokes party divisions is bad. The spirit of party is the implacable enemy of civic loyalty. Competition among parties is not, as some innocents would have it, a way of moderating or accommodating conflict; it is a form of civil war, and if left unchecked it can only be ended by the total victory and tyrannical rule of one party over all the others.

Second, political deliberations and civic decisions should be conducted openly, in the full gaze of all citizens. But political parties will have none of this. They plot their strategems and make their deals always in secret. Why? Because they must hide from public scrutiny their venality and their readiness to sacrifice principle for partisan advantage. If the parties' purposes were legitimate and their tactics respectable, they would have no need or desire for secrecy. Hence the secrecy is in itself proof of their evil intentions and subversive methods.[17]

Finally, no self-selected cabal should be allowed to intervene in the sovereign people's selection of their public officials. We have already seen traces of this idea in Robert La Follette and the Progressives, but one of its most uncompromising articulations was made by Thomas Hart Benton, the faithful Jacksonian Senator from Missouri. In a speech to the Senate in 1824 Benton attacked the

[17] See the attitudes described in George D. Luetscher, "Early Political Machinery in the United States" (Philadelphia: University of Pennsylvania Ph.D. thesis, 1903), pp. 60-62.

congressional caucus and all other forms of nominations by political parties. He reminded his colleagues that in the model republics of classical antiquity no such party intervention was needed or tolerated:

> Then the right of suffrage was enjoyed; the sovereignty of the people was no fiction. Then a sublime spectacle was seen, when the Roman citizen advanced to the polls and proclaimed, *"I vote for Cato to be Consul"*; the Athenian, *"I vote for Aristides to be Archon"* . . . And why may not an American do the same? Why may he not go up to the poll and proclaim, *"I vote for Thomas Jefferson to be President of the United States."*[18]

Benton's view was widely shared by Republicans and Federalists alike. The Federalists of Salem, Massachusetts, for example, issued a typical manifesto condemning the local Democratic Association and all "organized factions" for their "barefaced usurpation" of presuming "to dictate to the freemen thereof not only the Representatives in the Legislature but also every county and township officer."[19] In 1832 the Federalists' successors in the Illinois Senate passed a resolution deploring the new national party conventions despite their much-heralded improvement on the congressional caucus. Every person eligible for the presidency, the resolution said, has a right to be a candidate without the intervention of caucuses *or* conventions. Therefore, it concluded, "we disapprove of the system of conventions which Van Buren's party is endeavoring to thrust upon the American people, and we hold that this system is destructive of freedom of voting, con-

[18] Thomas Hart Benton, *Thirty Years' View* (New York: D. Appleton, 1854), Vol. I, pp. 39-40, emphasis in the original.
[19] Quoted in Luetscher, *op. cit.*, p. 93.

trary to republican institutions and dangerous to popular liberties."[20]

To the abolitionists, then, political parties are inherently and irremediably destructive of popular government. No internal reform or external restraint can make them any less so. The only way to preserve the republic against their subversion is to wipe them out. But how? Most abolitionists rejected Madison's view that the causes of party cannot be removed without destroying freedom of speech and assembly. The root cause of parties, some said, is the popular election of leading public officials; hence if we select those officials in some other manner, the parties will have nothing to organize and therefore nothing to feed on. Thus James Hillhouse, a Federalist U.S. Senator from Connecticut, argued in 1808 that

> [The office of President] serves as the rallying point of party. . . and cannot fail to bring forth and array all the electioneering artillery of the country; and furnish the most formidable means of organizing, concentrating, and cementing parties. And when a President shall be elected by means of party influence, thus powerfully exerted, he cannot avoid party bias, and will thence become the chief of a party, instead of taking the dignified attitude of a President of the United States. If some other mode of filling the Presidential chair than that of a general election throughout the United States were devised and adopted, it would be impossible to form national parties.[21]

[20] Quoted in M.I. Ostrogorski, *Democracy and the Organization of Political Parties*, translated from the French by Frederick Clarke (New York: Macmillan, 1902), Vol. II, p. 66. For other examples, see Hofstadter, *The Idea of a Party System*, p. 54.

[21] Quoted in Cunningham, *op. cit.*, p. 26. Luetscher quotes a similar arrgument against the popular election of governors made in the North Carolina constitutional convention of 1835: Luetscher, *op. cit.*, p. 113.

The remedy, Hillhouse concluded, is to return to the Founding Fathers' original design for choosing the President by an independent and unfactionalized Electoral College.

Thomas Hart Benton agreed with Hillhouse's diagnosis, but prescribed a different remedy. In 1824 and again in 1844 he proposed that since the electoral college had become hopelessly party-ridden, it should be abolished entirely and replaced by a system in which each congressional district's voters would freely express their choices for President, the candidate who got the most votes would win the district, and the candidate who won a majority of the districts would win the office. If no candidate got a majority on the first round, a run-off election would be held between the two candidates with the most districts. This, he believed, would eliminate parties and ensure the free and unmediated selection of the President by the people.[22]

But other people saw other ways. Some political leaders in the nation's early decades sought to eradicate parties by *using* rather than abolishing elections. Hofstadter reminds us that until the 1820s the party battle in America was

carried on in the face of a firm conviction by each side. . .that the other was not legitimate, and in a healthy state of affairs would be put out of business. . . . Each party hoped to bring about the other's destruction by devouring and absorbing as many of its more amenable followers as could be won over, and by forcing the remaining top leadership into disorganization and impotence.[23]

---

[22] Benton, *op. cit.*, Vol. I, p. 37; Vol. II, p. 627.
[23] Hofstadter, *The Idea of a Party System*, p. x; see also p. 8.

Ambivalence about Political Parties

Hofstadter shows that James Monroe was the most articulate advocate of the great strategem of achieving no-partyism through the triumph of one-partyism. Moreover, he believed that the strategem had finally succeeded in the "era of good feelings" over which he presided after the total collapse of the Federalist opposition after 1816.[24] But he was wrong. The Federalists' dissolution, his own nearly unanimous reelection, and the collapse of the congressional caucus led, not to the end of all political parties as Monroe expected, but to the emergence in the 1830s of what Richard McCormick has aptly called "the second American party system."[25]

But the revival of party competition did not obliterate Monroe's vision forever. In the two decades after the Civil War, a new generation of abolitionists arose. They are almost entirely forgotten today, but from the 1870s to the early 1900s they often appeared in the popular press with attacks on parties and proposals for their extermination.[26] The most widely published were Charles C.P. Clark, Nathan Cree, Albert Stickney, and James Sayles Brown. They all believed that the Republic was in mortal danger from the party warfare and corruption that bedeviled American affairs after Appomattox. Albert Stickney spoke for them all when he proclaimed that political parties were the basic disease. He was aware, he wrote, that some innocents hoped to cure the parties' evils by reforming them; but it was hopeless:

I believe. . . .that these evils. . .are not mere accidents, but that they are of the very essence of party;

[24] *Ibid.*, p. 196.

[25] Richard P. McCormick, *The Second American Party System* (Chapel Hill, N.C.: University of North Carolina Press, 1966).

[26] Their views are discussed in greater detail in my *The Doctrine of Responsible Party Government* (Urbana, Ill.: University of Illinois Press, 1954, 1962), p. 134.

that we cannot rid ourselves of these evils unless we rid ourselves of party; that what men call the good results of party we should still get if we had no parties; that party, instead of being a machinery necessary to the existence of free government, is its most dangerous foe; and that, in order to get anything which really deserves the name of republican government, we must destroy party altogether.[27]

The new abolitionists made various proposals for stamping out parties. Cree argued that, since parties are inevitable in any representative government, the only solution is to eliminate representation itself and place all lawmaking directly in the hands of the people through the initiative and referendum.[28] Stickney disagreed. Parties, he said, arise because of the recurring *elections* of representatives, not because of representation itself. Therefore, the solution is to end fixed terms of office. He proposed that the people should choose the legislators initially, that each legislator should stay in office as long as he performed satisfactorily, but that no legislator should be removed except for cause by the legislature itself, and that the legislature should select the members of the executive and judiciary. He pointed out that parties do not exist in the federal judiciary because it has no elections to be organized; so if we select all our officials in a similar manner the parties will disappear.[29]

But it was left to James Sayles Brown to pursue the abolitionist argument unflinchingly to its logical end. Let us not temporize with indirect and limited attacks on parties, he insisted; let us once and for all face the fact

[27] Albert Stickney, *A True Republic* (New York: Harper & Brothers, 1879), p. 104.

[28] Nathan Cree, *Direct Legislation by the People* (Chicago: A.C. McClurg, 1892).

[29] Stickney *op. cit.*, pp. 104, 151-152.

that the only cure for their evils is "a law declaring any candidate nominated by any such political organization ineligible to the office for which he is designated."[30] To be sure, he recognized, some will find such a proposal "extravagant and impracticable, if not altogether absurd." But its merits will be recognized by the

> large number of thoughtful and earnest citizens who cherish our free institutions, with the love which the fathers manifested for them, who see in the decay of public morals the degeneracy of our representative men, and in the increasing power of the political combinations which already rule and despoil us one of the greatest perils of the Republic.[31]

Now it is all very well for us in the 1970s to tut-tut the hyperbole of Brown's language and smile at the impracticality of his proposals. But we should recognize that echoes of his and the other abolitionists' view sounded prominently in the rhetoric and reforms of the Progressive era,[32] and they still echo today in the widespread antiparty sentiment we shall review in a moment. Neither Washington nor Benton nor Brown succeeded in abolishing parties; but they did much to thicken the atmosphere of contempt and distrust in which American parties have had to labor and in which party reforms have been debated from the 1790s to now. Their fondest hopes may have been disappointed, but their spirit liveth on.

THE DEFENDERS

Squarely opposed to the abolitionists have stood a succession of political analysts and leaders who have

---

[30] James Sayles Brown, *Partisan Politics: The Evil and the Remedy* (Philadelphia: J.B. Lippincott, 1897), p. 176.

[31] *Ibid*, p. 8.

[32] See, for example, Eugene C. Lee's description of the rationale

argued "that political parties created democracy and that modern democracy is unthinkable save in terms of the parties."[33] Even in the eighteenth century a few lonely voices were raised in praise of parties, although doing so must have been rather like praising the military-industrial complex or male chauvinism on American college campuses in the 1970s.

The most notable early defense of parties was made by Edmund Burke.[34] His argument survives today mainly because so many textbooks quote—disapprovingly—his definition of party as "a body of men united, for promoting by their joint endeavors the national interest upon some particular principles in which they are all agreed." But Burke's case was essentially an argument that *some* kind of political organization is necessary for the achievement of any political objective, and that the relatively large and open organizations of parties are greatly preferable to the relatively small and closed organizations of cliques, cabals, and what we today would call pressure groups. His defense of parties received little attention and less approval from his contemporary fellow intellectuals on either side of the Atlantic, and seems to have evoked even from his friends the sentiments expressed in the mock epitaph coined for him by Oliver Goldsmith:

---

underlying the establishment of nonpartisan elections for municipal offices in the Progressive era: *The Politics of Nonpartisanship* (Berkeley and Los Angeles: University of California Press, 1960), pp. 3, 18-24, 28-31.

[33] E.E. Schattschneider, *Party Government* (New York: Farrar and Rinehart, 1942), p. 1.

[34] Mainly in *Thoughts on the Cause of the Present Discontents* (1770), reprinted in Peter J. Stanlis (ed.), *Edmund Burke: Selected Writings and Speeches* (Garden City, N.Y.: Anchor Books, 1963), pp. 101-147. Burke's ideas are compared with leading antiparty notions in Harvey C. Mansfield, Jr., *Statesmanship and Party Government* (Chicago: University of Chicago Press, 1965).

Ambivalence about Political Parties

Here lies our good Edmund, whose genius was such
We scarcely can praise it, or blame it too much;
Who, born for the Universe, narrow'd his mind,
And to party gave up what was meant for mankind.[35]

Another early defense of parties was briefly heard in the American House of Representatives in 1798 when Robert Goodloe Harper, a Federalist congressman, likened the opposition of the two parties to competition in a public exhibition:

The public is the judge, the two parties are the combatants, and that party which possesses power must employ it properly, must conduct the Government wisely, in order to insure public approbation, and retain their power. In this contention, while the two parties draw different ways, a middle course is produced generally conformable to the public good.[36]

Richard Hofstadter has shown, however, that "the first fully articulate justification of the party as a competitive organization" was made by Martin Van Buren and his colleagues in the "Albany Regency" and the Jacksonian Democratic party from the 1820s on.[37] Hofstadter points out that Van Buren, William Marcy, Silas Wright, and the other organizers and defenders of party were not aristocratic planters like the Founding Fathers, but middle-class lawyers. They were schooled in the give-and-take of courtroom and caucus; they regarded their partisan opponents as legitimate competitors to be contended with, not as subversive conspirators to be stamped out; and they

---

[35] "Retaliation, a Poem," in *The Poems and Plays of Oliver Goldsmith* (London: J.M. Dent and Sons, 1910), p. 38.
[36] Quoted in Hofstadter, *The Idea of a Party System*, p. 37.
[37] *Ibid.*, p. viii.

proclaimed that competition between broadly based and open political parties was the best way to guarantee the responsiveness of the government to the people.[38]

Both as a political leader and as a political theorist, Van Buren achieved much: he masterminded Andrew Jackson's presidential campaign; he won the presidency for his chief and, ultimately, for himself; and he more than anyone revived the two-party competition whose demise Monroe had prematurely celebrated. By conceiving and carrying through the first Democratic national convention he helped bring order out of the chaos left by the collapse of the congressional caucus. And in his posthumous book *Inquiry into the Origin and Course of Political Parties in the United States*[39] he set forth the first full case ever made for the proposition that political parties make modern democratic government possible. Yet today few portraits of him hang in the offices of professors of political history or political theory, and he was little more honored in his own time. As one historian of the era explains, then as now Van Buren's reputation could not flourish in the prevailing atmosphere of ambivalence toward political parties and those who praise them and do their work:

> Martin Van Buren was one of the new young career men of American politics, men whose reputation and success had grown largely within the bounds of organized party activity. *Americans liked party maneuvers as they liked heady, precarious ventures in land and business; they deeply honored neither.* In Van Buren for the first time a President appeared who had no

---

[38] *Ibid.*, pp. 209-210, 216, 224-225, 239-242, 244-252. See also Michael Wallace, "Changing Concepts of Party in the United States: New York, 1815-1828," *American Historical Review*, 74 (December, 1968), 453-491.

[39] Martin Van Buren, *Inquiry into the Origins and Course of Political Parties in the United States*, edited by his sons (New York: Hurd and Houghton, 1867).

ennobling ties with the Founding Fathers, who had not lost or shed blood in the national cause, whose remembered past included no battlefields but the courtroom and the back room. A second-rate old man beat him in 1840 with a contrived log cabin and a real battlefield.[40]

Most of Van Buren's successors in defending parties have not had their ideas or reputations tested in quite the same way as his, for most have been academics. They include Francis Lieber, Professor of History and Political Science at Columbia in the mid-nineteenth century; Henry Jones Ford, Professor of Politics at Princeton at the turn of the century; A. Lawrence Lowell, Professor of Government and President of Harvard in the early twentieth century; and, in the past three decades, Herbert Agar, Pendleton Herring of Harvard, Clinton Rossiter of Cornell, and Nelson Polsby and Aaron Wildavsky of Berkeley.[41] These defenders have praised the parties' contributions to the moderation of conflict and the nurturing of consensus, and most have concluded that any radical change in the parties' existing structures or competitive relationships would cripple their ability to aggregate interests and cool conflict. It is not clear what impact the academic defenders of party have had on the course of

[40] Marvin Meyers, *The Jacksonian Persuasion: Politics and Belief* (Stanford, Calif.: Stanford University Press, 1957), p. 113, emphasis added.

[41] Lieber's ideas are discussed in Hofstadter, *The Idea of a Party System*, pp. 257-259; and Lowell's and Ford's in my *The Doctrine of Responsible Party Government*, Chs. 4-5. For the others, see: Herbert Agar, *The Price of Union* (Boston: Houghton Mifflin, 1950); Pendleton Herring, *The Politics of Democracy* (New York: W.W. Norton, 1940, 1965); Clinton Rossiter, *Parties and Politics in America* (Ithaca, N.Y.: Cornell University Press, 1960); and Nelson W. Polsby and Aaron B. Wildavsky, *Presidential Elections* (3rd ed., New York: Charles Scribner's Sons, 1971), esp. Chs. 4-5. The same view is advanced in Ranney and Kendall, *op. cit.*, esp. Chs. 21-22.

events, but they have at least won some converts among the authors of college textbooks.[42] They have had less success with the authors of high school civics textbooks. Perhaps the greatest impact any academic can hope for is convincing other academics; but some have refused to settle for so modest a goal.

THE REFORMERS

Many academic party-watchers and a few political leaders have taken a third view. American parties, they say, are potentially the key to truly democratic and effective government, but as they now exist they are indeed guilty of many of the changes leveled against them by the abolitionists. Therefore it is equally wrong to abolish parties or to leave them as they are. The thing to do is reform them. And there has been no lack of proposals for doing just that, although some of them are quite incompatible with others.

One group of reformers, generally called the "responsible party government" school, has included such academic notables as Woodrow Wilson, Frank Goodnow, E.E. Schattschneider, Stephen Bailey, James MacGregor Burns, and the members of the American Political Science Association's 1950 Committee on Political Parties.[43] These writers have generally argued that parties will never play their proper role in the American system until they become centralized, disciplined, and cohesive national bodies dedicated to formulating, expounding, and implementing policy programs. The perceptive analysis of this school's political theory by Polsby and Wildavsky concludes that to such reformers the best political parties are

[42] For example, Ranney and Kendall, *op. cit.*
[43] Their views are discussed at length in my *The Doctrine of Responsible Party Government*, Chs. 1-3, 6, 9-10.

parties which 1) make policy commitments to the electorate, 2) are willing and able to carry them out when in office, 3) develop alternatives to government policies when out of office, and 4) differ sufficiently between themselves to "provide the electorate with a proper range of choice between alternatives of action."[44]

The doctrine of responsible party government received considerable attention from academic political scientists in the period from 1890 to 1915. After World War I it was hardly mentioned until the publication of Schattschneider's *Party Government* in 1942. His revival of the doctrine fired the imaginations of a number of political scientists, especially those most disappointed by Franklin D. Roosevelt's failure to convert the Democratic party into a cohesive force united behind liberal programs. The reborn movement grew so strong that in 1946 the American Political Science Association appointed a prestigious sixteen-member Committee on Political Parties to study and report on "the condition and improvement of national party organization," and named Schattschneider as chairman.

In 1950 the Committee published its report, entitled "Toward a More Responsible Two-Party System." Its theories and recommendations touched off a debate that has shaped much of the academic discussion of parties ever since. In Chapter 1 we noted the report's leading advocates and critics and outlined some arguments of each side. We should recognize here that one of the critics' most telling points was their declaration that, regardless of how enthusiastic college professors might be about the report's prescriptions, party politicians and the man in the street showed no interest whatever, let alone the kind of fervor

[44] Polsby and Wildavsky, *op. cit.*, p. 225.

needed to make possible such sweeping changes. Hence, argued the critics, regardless of their merits the reforms simply were not going to be made.

As one who made this point in the debate's early years,[45] I find it intriguing to add up the score today, a quarter-century after the report's publication, to see what impact, if any, it has had upon the course of events outside the ivory tower. Hence in Table 1 I have listed the report's specific recommendations for internal party reform and recorded my judgment about where each of them stands in early 1974.

The observations in Table 1 add up to some movement by the parties toward the Committee's goals since 1950, but not much.[46] Their score will improve somewhat if the Democrats' 1974 Conference on Party Organization and Policy adopts a structure similar to the one proposed jointly in 1972 by the McGovern-Fraser and O'Hara commissions, but whether the Conference will or will not remains to be seen.[47]

Whatever may be the responsible-party reformers' ultimate impact, however, it is clear that much greater clout has been exercised by quite a different group of reformers, whom we may call the "representative party structures" school. They have argued that, contrary to the Schattsch-

[45] Mainly in "Toward a More Responsible Two-Party System: A Commentary," *American Political Science Review*, 45 (June 1951), 488-499, esp. at 498-499.

[46] Evron M. Kirkpatrick, a member of the original Committee, comes to the same conclusion in his retrospective analysis of the report: "'Toward a More Responsible Two-Party System': Political Science, Policy Science, or Pseudo-Science?", *American Political Science Review*, 65 (December 1971), 965-990. Gerald M. Pomper, on the other hand, argues that events are moving much as the Committee desired or predicted: "Toward a More Responsible Two-Party System: What, Again?", *Journal of Politics*, 33 (November 1971), 916-940.

[47] The commissions' proposed charter will be discussed in Chapter 5.

TABLE 1
1973 STATUS OF THE RECOMMENDATIONS OF
THE APSA's 1950 COMMITTEE ON POLITICAL PARTIES

Recommendation	Status[a]
1. National Conventions	
hold every two years	char
have fewer delegates and alternates	opp
2. National Committees	
convention more active in selection of members	Dem
members reflect party strength of areas they represent	Dem
have larger permanent professional staffs	Rep
3. Establish Party Councils of 50 Members, with Power to:	
adopt platforms	char
make recommendations about congressional candidates	no
discipline state and local parties deserting national party program	no
4. Platforms	
party councils to adopt and interpret	char
considered binding on all party officeholders at all levels	no
state party platforms adopted after national platform	no
adopted every two years	char
members of Congress to participate more actively in writing	char
state and local platforms made to conform to national	no
5. Congressional Parties	
consolidate all Senate and House leadership positions into a single effective leadership committee	no
more frequent caucus meetings	no
caucus decisions on legislative policy binding on members	no
no committee chairmanships by seniority for opponents of party programs	no
replace control of legislative calendar by Rules Committee with control by party leadership committee	no
6. Nominations	
closed primaries	Dem
no cross-filing	both
more preprimary conventions	opp
national presidential primary	no

[a] *Legend:*
  both—adopted by both parties
  Dem—adopted by Democratic party only
  Rep—adopted by Republican party only
  char—proposed in 1972 proposed Democratic national charter
  no—not adopted by either party
  opp—movement in the opposite direction by one or both parties

Source: The specific recommendations are in "Toward a More Responsible Two-Party System," *American Political Science Review,* 44 (September, 1950, supplement), pp. 5–10.

neider school's view, the parties' greatest need is not more centralization or cohesion but more accurate *representation* of their rank-and-file members. Their views prevailed in the McGovern-Fraser commission and strongly influenced the Republicans' DO Committee as well. In Chapters 4 and 5 we shall consider in detail the theory and practice of the many changes they have wrought.

Finally, there is yet a third group of reformers, which has been most influential of all. I shall call them the "regulators." They include some of our most powerful political leaders, from James Madison to Mike Mansfield, who have felt that the "mischiefs of faction" can be cured only by imposing strict legal regulations. Like Madison they have accepted the proposition that parties are inevitable in a representative government that cherishes free speech and assembly. To be sure, some have expressed this acceptance grudgingly in terms that sound rather like resigning oneself to the fact of original sin. For example, M.I. Ostrogorski, the turn-of-the-century Russian scholar and critic of American and British parties, said there is no point in studying *why* parties arise in human affairs:

> The historian who should turn his investigations in this direction might as well undertake to write the history of human deceit or human spite. One would not have to begin with the time of the [American] Revolution; one could trace the origin of the caucus to a date far anterior. To be precise, the beginning would have to be carried back to the garden of Eden, where the first caucus was held by Eve and the serpent.[48]

[48] M.I. Ostrogorski, "The Rise and Fall of the Nominating Caucus, Legislative and Congressional," *American Historical Review*, 5 (December, 1899), 254.

Ambivalence about Political Parties

But whatever may be their views about why parties arise, the regulators have agreed on three propositions. First, left to their own devices parties will continue to work mischief. Second, they cannot be abolished without sacrificing freedom of speech and assembly, which is too great a price to pay. So, third, parties must be regulated by law because the only agency powerful enough to keep them under control is the state.

The great impact of the regulators on the life of American parties becomes apparent when we compare their status with that of their counterparts in other Western nations. As we shall see in Chapter 3, in every other modern democratic polity except West Germany, political parties are largely or entirely unknown to the law, and they control their own memberships, choice of leaders, formulation of programs, and selection of candidates with little or no supervision by parliaments, courts, or bureaucrats. In the United States, on the other hand, ever since the last decade of the nineteenth century our state and local parties have operated under severe restrictions imposed by elaborate legal codes that govern every aspect of their affairs. And today debate over the status of parties centers on the issue of whether legal regulation should be fully extended to the national parties.

It is clear, then, that the doctrines of the reformers in general and the regulators in particular have long been and continue to be the most influential of the three attitudes toward parties held by American political and intellectual leaders. Yet one of the main theses of this book is that the reformers have had their way so often mainly because they have operated in a political culture which supports the attitude that, while parties have to be tolerated, they must be regulated—not encouraged or left alone. I shall conclude this chapter by reviewing what

47

is known about how ordinary Americans feel about these matters.

ATTITUDES TOWARD PARTIES: THE PEOPLE

In this chapter, as in those to follow, we focus mainly on party and reform leaders rather than on mass publics because the leaders' ideas and maneuvers are the proximate causes for the events we seek to understand. Yet we should not ignore entirely the attitudes of ordinary Americans. After all, their support, opposition, or indifference provides many of the conditions for the leaders' conflicts over party reform and in a general way controls their outcomes. In this sense there is much to be said for Schattschneider's view, quoted in Chapter 1, that if a substantial number of citizens were to demand centralized and disciplined parties they would probably get them without there being any need to make a lot of formal changes in the Constitution or the statutes.[49] But that argument works just as well the other way around; if most of the mass public values independence in its public officials and prefers that no party organization be allowed to become too powerful, then the prospects for responsible party government—though not necessarily for other kinds of party reform—will be dim.

Ordinary Americans do not write books or give public lectures, so we have much less direct evidence on how they have felt about parties than about how their leaders have felt. In the past forty years, however, public opinion polls have told us something about how our contemporaries feel, and it is worth summarizing what we have learned.

[49] See Schattschneider's statement quoted on p. 7 above.

Ambivalence about Political Parties

PARTY IDENTIFICATION V. APPROVAL
OF PARTIES AS INSTITUTIONS

The first point to note is that about two-thirds of American adults are to some degree "party identifiers"—that is, they feel some measure of preference for one party over the others. Since 1940 the American Institute of Public Opinion has been asking its national samples the question on the same point: First, "Generally speaking, a Republican, Democrat, or Independent?" The largest proportion ever claiming to be Independents was 33 percent in 1973, and the mean has been 26 percent.[50]

Using a somewhat more sophisticated approach, the Survey Research Center (SRC) of the University of Michigan has since 1952 asked its national samples a *two-step* question on the same point, First, "Generally speaking, do you usually think of yourself as a Republican, a Democrat, an independent, or what?" Second, those mentioning a party are then asked, "Would you say that you are a strong or not so strong (Republican/Democrat)?"; and those replying "independent" to the first question are asked, "In general, do you consider yourself closer to the Republican or to the Democratic party?" This technique allows all respondents to be classified as strong partisans, weak partisans, independent leaners, or independents. It has been used in every even-numbered year since 1952; the results in presidential election years from 1960 to 1972 are summarized in Table 2.

The data in Table 2 show that since 1960 the SRC has never found that less than 64 percent of their respondents were party identifiers. The mean has been 72 percent—a figure very close to Gallup's mean of 74 percent. Moreover,

[50] *Congressional Quarterly Weekly Report*, September 15, 1973, p. 2469.

TABLE 2
AMERICAN PARTY IDENTIFICATIONS, 1960–1972
(in percent)

Identification	1960	1964	1968	1972
Strong Democrat	21	27	20	15
Weak Democrat	25	25	25	26
Independent Democrat	8	9	10	11
Independent	8	8	11	13
Independent Republican	7	6	9	10
Weak Republican	13	13	14	13
Strong Republican	14	11	10	10
Apolitical	4	1	1	2
	100	100	100	100

Source: Survey Research Center, University of Michigan, furnished through the Inter-University Consortium for Political Research.

the SRC has never found more than 13 percent expressing no party preference of any degree, and the mean has been 10 percent.[51]

However, Table 2 also reveals a recent development that may change the whole picture. Since 1964 the proportion of Strong Democrats has declined by almost half (27 percent to 15 percent), the proportion of Independents with no party leanings has nearly doubled (8 percent to 13 percent), and the proportion of Independents who have some party leanings has also risen sharply (15 percent to 21 percent.)

So the symptoms are clear: for the moment, at least, more Americans are calling themselves "independents" than at any time since modern public opinion polls began. The political diagnosticians, however, disagree about what is producing these symptoms. Walter Dean Burnham, for instance, believes they show a general and perhaps irreversible decline in the importance of parties in Americans'

[51] The distributions for the years prior to 1970 are given in Hugh A. Bone and Austin Ranney, *Politics and Voters* (3d ed., New York: McGraw-Hill, 1971), Table 1, p. 9. The figures for 1972 have been furnished by the Inter-University Consortium for Political Research.

minds and thus in the nation's political life.[52] In 1970 former Senator and presidential aspirant Eugene Mc-Carthy was sure the Gallup figures meant that a growing number of Americans are dissatisfied with the old parties and long for a new party of the sort he himself might lead.[53] Nelson W. Polsby, on the other hand, reminds us of the well-established fact that young people have always called themselves "independents" in much larger proportions than older people,[54] and suggests that the recent overall increase in self-styled "independents" is mainly a reflection of the increasing proportion of young people in the electorate.[55] And E.M. Schreiber finds that the increase comes in part from persons under thirty but mainly from white southerners of all ages who have really become

[52] ."The End of American Party Politics," *Trans-action*, 7 (December, 1969), 12-22.

[53] "A Third Party May Be a Real Force in '72," *New York Times Magazine*, June 7, 1970. No such party was formed in 1972, and almost all of McCarthy's 1968 supporters deserted him for George McGovern and remained in the Democratic party. This prompted some observers to describe McCarthy, perhaps cruelly, as "a man for one season"; but his argument that a left-oriented third or fourth party is imminent has survived his own political career.

[54] See, for example, the SRC's findings for the 1950s reported in Angus Campbell, Philip E. Converse, Warren E. Miller, and Donald E. Stokes, *The American Voter* (New York: John Wiley & Sons, 1960), pp. 161-165. In 1970 Jack Dennis and I found that the proportion of self-styled independents is highest of all among college students: our survey of 2,845 college students revealed that fully 75 percent regarded themselves as independents or independent leaners, compared with only 31 percent in the general population and only 44 percent in the noncollege 21-30 age group. We also found that 30 percent of the students expressed no preference whatever for either party, com. pared with 13 percent in the general population and 18 percent in the noncollege 21-30 group. Part of the study, though not these data, is reported in Jack Dennis and Austin Ranney. "Working Within the System: Academic Recess and College Student Participation in the 1970 Elections," *American Politics Quarterly*, 1 (January, 1973), 93-124.

[55] Nelson W. Polsby, "An Emerging Republican Majority?", *The Public Interest*, 14 (Fall, 1969), 119-126.

Republican identifiers but are not yet willing to say so publicly.[56]

For many political scientists this is an absorbing and complex problem, but it need detain us here no longer. For our purposes the important point is that most Americans still prefer one party or the other to some degree, and in that sense are partisans. We also know that people's partisan preferences tell us quite a bit about how they are likely to act politically. For example, the more partisan they are the more likely they are to vote, to choose their party's presidential candidate, and to vote the straight party ticket. Nevertheless, the 1972 Nixon landslide, combined with the Democrats' considerable victories in elections for Congress and for state offices, again makes it perfectly clear that a significant number of partisans often vote for some of the opposition party's candidates, especially in such highly visible contests as those for President, governor, and U.S. Senator.[57]

But from here on our argument must proceed very carefully. Whatever partisanship may mean for voting behavior, we cannot conclude that a person's preference for one party over the other means that he approves of parties *in general* as desirable institutions. After all, Alexander Hamilton was a fiercely partisan Federalist and James Monroe an equally partisan Republican; yet both abominated parties and party conflict, and each looked forward to the day his party's total victory would end *all* parties, including his own. And ordinary people are surely entitled to be as ambivalent as their leaders about partisanship and parties. So we need more direct evidence

[56] E.M. Schreiber, "'Where the Ducks Are': Southern Strategy versus Fourth Party," *Public Opinion Quarterly*, 35 (Summer, 1971), 164-165.

[57] The point is made in many studies. See especially Campbell, Converse, Miller, and Stokes, *op. cit.*, pp. 136-139; and William H. Flanigan, *Political Behavior of the American Electorate* (Boston: Allyn and Bacon, 1968), pp. 33-38.

than the incidence of party identification to tell us how Americans feel about the institution of parties. Fortunately, at least some such evidence is available.

THE PEOPLE'S "IDEA OF A PARTY SYSTEM"

Several public opinion studies have tapped ordinary Americans' attitudes toward the institution of political parties and party politicians. For example, in 1973 the Gallup Poll repeated a question it had asked several times before: "If you had a son, would you like to see him go into politics as a life's work?" A whopping 64 percent replied "No," only 23 percent said "Yes," and the remainder had no opinion.[58] For another example, the National Opinion Research Center found in the mid-1940s that most people had a low opinion of "politicians": politics, they felt, almost obliges politicians to be self-seeking, hypocritical, and corrupt. On the other hand, most had a high opinion of elected public officials.[59] What are we to make of this? Is it good to be an elected official, but bad to do the organizing and campaigning necessary to win office? It seems inconsistent and unfair; yet one is reminded of the venerable tradition that "the office should seek the man" and not vice-versa.

In 1969 *Newsweek* magazine tackled the question from another angle. They asked a national sample to rate the performance of various American institutions as "excellent," "good," or "poor," and compiled composite ratings for each. Political parties finished dead last: only 18 percent of the respondents rated them "excellent" or "good," as compared with 68 percent for universities, 56 percent for business, 33 percent for organized religion,

[58] Reported in the Milwaukee *Journal*, July 13, 1973, p. 5.
[59] William C. Mitchell, "The Ambivalent Social Status of the American Politician," *Western Political Quarterly*, 12 (September, 1959), 683-698.

and—the unkindest cut of all—40 percent for the police.[60]

But the most direct and thorough investigation yet made of this topic is Jack Dennis's study of the attitudes of Wisconsin adults made in 1964, at a time when people's party identifications were probably stronger than they are now.[61] Dennis found that only 10 percent of his respondents expressed no preference for any party; 30 percent were strong identifiers, 42 percent were weak identifiers, and 18 percent were independent leaners. Thus his respondents were, if anything, somewhat more partisan than Americans in general. But then Dennis presented them with a series of statements praising and criticizing various aspects of the party system, and asked them to agree or disagree. Their replies—especially when considered in the light of their partisanship—show an ambivalence toward parties as institutions strikingly similar to that which we have previously observed in so many American political and intellectual leaders. The replies are arrayed in Table 3, and they show that one can support a particular party and still take a dim view of the *institution* of parties.

On the basis of the replies in Table 3, we can summarize the popular attitude toward political parties as follows. Parties do not merely reflect political conflict, they create it. This conflict hurts the country more than it helps, in part because it makes the government less efficient. The good citizen should always vote for the individual candidate, not the party; yet it is good to have party labels on the ballot. Strong party competition helps democracy work, and people who serve parties during campaigns do the nation a good service. On the other hand, the citizen has no obligation to give money to his party, and no tax deductions should be allowed to people who do. Parties

[60] *Newsweek*, December 29,.1969, p. 43.
[61] Jack Dennis, "Support for the Party System by the Mass Public," *American Political Science Review*, 60 (September, 1966), 600-615.

Ambivalence about Political Parties

TABLE 3
ATTITUDES OF WISCONSIN ADULTS TOWARD POLITICAL PARTIES

Statement	Percent responding			
	Agree	Dis-agree	Mixed	Don't Know
Parties as Fomenters of Social Conflict				
"The conflicts and controversies between the parties hurt our country more than they help it."	47	35	14	4
"Our system of government would work a lot more efficiently if we could get rid of conflicts between the parties altogether."	53	34	8	5
"The political parties more often than not create conflicts where none really exists."	64	15	13	8
"Democracy works best where competition between parties is strong."	68	12	12	8
Parties as Agencies Deserving Popular Support				
"The best rule in voting is to pick the man regardless of his party label."	82	10	6	2
"It would be better if, in all elections, we put no party labels on the ballot."	22	67	7	4
"People who work for parties during political campaigns do our nation a great service."	68	10	19	4
"Even if people are not able to help their political parties in other ways, they ought to contribute money to the party of their choice."	28	50	18	3
"Tax deductions should be allowed for people who contribute money to the political party of their choice."	19	68	7	6
Responsible Party Government				
"The parties do more to confuse the issues than to provide a clear choice on them."	54	21	19	6
"Things would be better if the parties took opposite stands on issues more than they do now."	31	43	17	10
"We would be better off if all the Democrats in government stood together and all the Republicans did the same."	30	54	12	5
"A senator or representative should follow his party leaders even if he doesn't want to."	23	63	9	5
"Our senators and representatives ought to follow their party leaders more than they do."	41	33	20	7

Source: Jack Dennis, "Support for the Party System by the Mass Public," *American Political Science Review,* 60 (September, 1966), 600–615.

confuse rather than clarify the issues, but things would not be better if they took more opposed stands than they do now.[62] Things would not be improved if the parties became more cohesive. Elected public officials should not follow their party leaders if they do not want to—but it would be better if they did so more than they now do.[63]

From this evidence we can conclude only that most ordinary Americans share their leaders' ambivalence about political parties. Most prefer one party to the others, at least to some degree; most have many hostile and few supportive feelings about the existing party system; but most do not want it abolished or converted into a British-style "responsible party" government. Indeed, as one tries to epitomize just how American's leaders and followers feel about political parties, one is reminded of Mr. Dooley's characterization of how Theodore Roosevelt felt about the trusts:

> "Th' thrusts," says he, "are heejous monsthers built up be th' enlightened intherprise iv th' men that have done so much to advance progress in our beloved country," he says. "On wan hand I wud stamp thim undher fut; on th' other hand not so fast."[64]

One thing is sure: in our time, just as in Madison's and La Follette's, America's political and intellectual leaders

[62] This confirms the findings of earlier studies that most Americans do not want a party realignment that would put all the liberals in one party and all the conservatives in the other: cf. George H. Smith and Richard P. Davis, "Do the Voters Want the Parties Changed?", *Public Opinion Quarterly*, 11 (Summer, 1947), 236-243.

[63] The lack of enthusiasm for party cohesion and discipline of maverick congressmen was also found by studies in 1938 (Roper), 1946 (Gallup), and 1958 (SRC): see Donald J. Devine, *The Political Culture of the United States* (Boston: Little, Brown, 1972), pp. 174-176.

[64] Quoted in Henry F. Pringle, *Theodore Roosevelt: A Biography* (New York: Harcourt, Brace, 1931), p. 245.

Ambivalence about Political Parties

are not fettered by any iron public will to abolish, preserve, or reform the parties. The public's ambivalence leaves them free to deal with parties as their own ambivalences may prompt. How they and their predecessors have used that freedom, and with what consequences for the American way of politics, is our concern in the chapters to follow.

CHAPTER THREE

Putting the Parties
in Their Place

Any effort to understand the politics of one time from the perspective of another is hazardous, and our own survey of the theory and practice of party reform in America is no exception. One hazard is that, as we review and evaluate what Americans in earlier times have said and done about party reform, we assume that they saw what they were doing as just as important as we see it, and for the same reasons.

But the fact is that until well after the Civil War most Americans—even those most involved in the early conflicts over party reform—thought they were dealing with passing matters of practical necessity rather than with matters eternally central to the life of the Republic. To be sure, many reforms were adopted which we now regard as highly important: for example, the end of nominations by legislative and congressional caucuses in the 1820s, the creation of the national nominating conventions in the 1830s, and the establishment of the national committees in the 1840s. But the people who instituted those reforms did so almost casually, believing them to be useful solutions to practical problems, not matters of high principle. And their ideas and actions received no attention whatever from James Kent, Theodore Parker, Alexis de Tocqueville, Henry David Thoreau, or the period's other leading commentators.[1]

There is no mystery about why this was so. Until well after the Civil War parties were not generally thought to be either permanent or important features of the nation's political life, and there seemed no reason why serious men should pay serious attention to sordid little intraparty squabbles. On the rare occasions when the organization of parties was mentioned in the course of official government business, most respectable people found the topic demeaning to the dignity of the forum. For example, in March, 1824 there was some discussion on the floor of the United States Senate about whether the Republican party's congressional caucus should continue to make presidential nominations. Almost every Senator present had personally participated in making such nominations, but most who spoke regretted that so unsuitable a topic had been raised in official debate. Walter Lowrie of Pennsylvania said, "It is with a sensation of pain that I observe the situation in which the Senate is. . .placed by introducing the subject." John Henry Eaton of Tennessee declared that the topic was "altogether improper" and "ought not to be permitted to remain any longer before the Senate." It was, he said, "unbecoming the dignity of the body," and would "place the members in no very elevated view before the public." And William Findlay of Pennsylvania

[1] Cf. Marvin Meyers' statement that in the 1820s and 1830s "the most consequential changes entered silently, without formal consideration or enactment: changes in the organization and conduct of parties": *The Jacksonian Persuasion* (Stanford, Calif.: Stanford University Press, 1957), p. 4. See also James Staton Chase, "Jacksonian Democracy and the Rise of the Nominating Convention," *Mid-America: An Historical Review*, 45 (October, 1963), 248-249.

ended the embarrassment by declaring that "as this [is] the most unpleasant discussion. . .[I] have ever heard since [I] have had the honor of a seat in the Senate, [I will] endeavor to terminate it"—which he did by successfully moving to adjourn.[2] So it seems that in the Era of Good Feelings political necessity might occasionally force one to *practice* party politics, but simple etiquette required one at least not to *talk* about it in the Republic's highest tribunals.

By the 1870s, however, most politicians and political commentators accepted the fact that, for better or worse, parties had become an established part of the nation's political life.[3] One consequence was a veritable quantum jump in the volume of comment about how the parties operated and might be purified. Another was the rapid growth of a notion that has profoundly affected the parties ever since: the idea that they will not voluntarily mend their ways and so must legally be forced to behave. When that notion became widespread in the 1880s, conflict over party reform became highly visible and discussion of it even respectable. It has remained so ever since.

RULES, STAKES, AND OUTCOMES IN PARTY REFORM

The immediate object of dispute over party reform in all epochs has been the *rules*—the party rules, public laws, or both governing the status, organization, membership, and operations of the parties. As in all conflicts over rules,

[2] Thomas Hart Benton (ed.), *Abridgment of the Debates of Congress, from 1789 to 1856* (New York: D. Appleton, 1858), Vol. VII, pp. 523, 529, 534.

[3] Cf. Austin Ranney, "The Reception of Political Parties into American Political Science," *Southwestern Social Science Quarterly*, 32 (December, 1951), 183-191; and Richard Hofstadter, *The Idea of a Party System* (Berkeley, Los Angeles and London: University of California Press, 1969), Ch. 6.

most of the debates have consisted of arguments over normative issues of what values should be maximized in the political system, and over empirical issues of what institutional arrangements are likely to maximize the preferred values. The debaters have touched on many of political theory's most ancient and difficult questions, and we shall pay full heed to what they have said.

While doing so, however, we should bear in mind the truism that decisions on rules are never politically neutral. Any rule governing the conduct of conflict is bound to make the competition easier for some contestants and more difficult for others. So any proposal to change a rule is in part a proposal to alter each contestant's chances for success. Thus the politics of party reform, like any other kind of politics, is bound to be, in Harold Lasswell's famous phrase, a contest over "who gets what, when, how."[4]

We shall review many arguments about the merits of particular party reforms as judged by the standards of democracy, representativeness, participation, and other abstract ideals. What I said a moment ago does not mean that these arguments have been uttered only by knaves or fools. It does mean that in each dispute there has been more at stake than the logical proximity of words in a rule to words in a statement of high principle. And it also means that to understand fully any particular conflict over party reform we must consider not only what the contestants said but also who they were and what they stood to gain or lose by the reform in dispute. For, as Paul David

[4] Harold D. Lasswell, *Politics: Who Gets What, When, How* (New York: McGraw-Hill, 1936). A sample of other expositions of this view are: Robert A. Dahl, *Modern Political Analysis* (Englewood Cliffs, N.J.: Prentice-Hall, 1963), Ch. 7; David B. Truman, *The Governmental Process* (2nd ed., New York: Alfred A. Knopf, 1971), Ch. V; and Austin Ranney, *The Governing of Men* (3d ed., New York: Holt, Rinehart, and Winston, 1971), Ch. 1.

and his colleagues concluded in their massive survey of the national nominating conventions:

> Changes in party rules seem most likely to occur when a proposal of seeming general merit happens to coincide with the factional interests of a potential majority group that needs an issue.[5]

The relevance of this observation for party reform can be shown by a brief review of battles over reforms in the parties' procedures for nominating presidential candidates.

DEVELOPMENT OF NOMINATIONS BY LEGISLATIVE AND CONGRESSIONAL CAUCUSES

1. *The State Legislative Caucus System.* In America's preparty days, prior to the early 1790s, most nominations of candidates for elective offices were made by self-presentation: the aspirant simply announced through the newspapers or on the town bulletin board that he was seeking the office. In a few areas, nominations were occasionally made by mass meetings and even by primitive delegate conventions; but self-presentation was by far the most common method.[6] This was the Golden Age looked back on so longingly by those commentators, mentioned in Chapter 1, who condemned nominations by parties on the ground that no self-selected body should intervene between the sovereign people and their choice of public officials.

[5] Paul T. David, Ralph M. Goldman, and Richard C. Bain, *The Politics of National Party Conventions* (Washington, D.C.: Brookings Institution, 1960), p. 191.

[6] George D. Luetscher, "Early Political Machinery in the United States" (Philadelphia: University of Pennsylvania Ph.D. Thesis, 1903), pp. 63-66; and M.I. Ostrogorski, *Democracy and the Organization of Political Parties*, translated from the French by Frederick Clarke (New York: Macmillan, 1902), Vol. II, pp. 3-10.

Putting the Parties in Their Place

But the Golden Age did not last very long. When the parties began to emerge in the early 1790s their prime object was to concert their strength behind selected candidates so as to maximize their chances of winning elections. Hence each party's first organizational need was a procedure for selecting its candidates, identifying them to the voters as the party's standard-bearers, and uniting the party's adherents behind them in the campaign. They generally settled upon what was called a "caucus" or "primary": the terms were used interchangeably to mean a general meeting of all of a town's or county's party supporters who cared to attend. Such meetings were called "primaries" not only because they occurred earlier in time than the general elections but also because they were thought to be closest to the parties' members.[7]

At first the parties' nominees for such statewide offices as governor and lieutenant governor were chosen by caucuses held in the state's capital city, to which partisans from all parts of the state were nominally invited. But the difficulties of eighteenth century transportation prevented most nonresidents from attending, and the primaries were dominated by residents of the capital. This struck most nonresidents as highly unfair, and some unsung Solon thought up a solution: the party's members in the state legislature came from all parts of the state; their nomination and election proved they had the confidence of the people in their districts; and they were already resident in the capital. Therefore, they should pick the party's nominees for statewide offices on behalf of the party's members in the whole state. This suggestion made good sense to most partisans, and by 1800 both parties' nominations for governor and lieutenant governor in most states were made by their legislative caucuses.[8]

[7] Luetscher, *op. cit.*, pp. 66-67.

[8] Frederick W. Dallinger, *Nominations for Elective Office in the*

Soon thereafter a number of the party faithful in legislative districts held by the opposition party complained that since they had no legislator to speak for them they were unrepresented in the nominating machinery. Thus the parties for the first time faced the issue of the apportionment of party assemblies which has plagued them ever since, as we shall see later in this chapter. In the early 1800s the parties dealt with it by instituting what came to be known as "mixed caucuses." These were gatherings in the capital not only of the party's legislators but also of delegates elected by caucuses in those districts that had no party legislator.[9] As we shall see, the mixed caucuses were the precursors of the delegate conventions which became the dominant nominating method a generation later.

2. *Origins of the Congressional Caucus Nominating System.*[10] From the mid-1790s on the Republican and Federalist members of Congress met together occasionally in caucuses to discuss issues and plot legislative strategy. It is not clear just when these bodies first began to nominate their parties' presidential candidates, but most historians agree that both parties held nominating caucuses in 1800. Ironically, the first appears to have been called by Alexander Hamilton, the archenemy of the whole idea of organized party competition. Whatever his feeling about parties, Hamilton had a practical problem needing an immediate solution. He felt that John Adams would make a feeble showing against Thomas Jefferson, and he calculated that Charles Cotesworth Pinckney could beat

United States (New York: Longmans, Green, 1897), pp. 25-27; Ostrogorski, *op. cit.*, pp. 10-11.

[9] Ostrogorski, *op. cit.*, pp. 35-37.

[10] The account in the text is drawn mainly from Dallinger, *op. cit.*, pp. 13-16; Ostrogorski, *op. cit.*, pp. 13-15; and Richard P. McCormick, *The Second American Party System* (Chapel Hill, N.C.: University of North Carolina Press, 1966), pp. 24-26.

Adams for the nomination and perhaps also Jefferson in the election. But Adams was the incumbent President and thus the likely choice of most Federalist electors. Since at that time, prior to the adoption of the Twelfth Amendment, each member of the Electoral College voted for two persons, Hamilton's strategy was to persuade the Federalists to concert their strength behind Pinckney as well as Adams—in the hope that Pinckney would ultimately get more votes than Adams and be elected Vice President if not President. So he persuaded the Federalist members of Congress to meet secretly in the Senate chamber and recommend—"nominate," we would say—Adams and Pinckney.[11] The Republicans met in the same year in less formal surroundings—Marache's boarding house in Philadelphia—and endorsed Jefferson for President and Aaron Burr for Vice President.

After the election of 1800 the Federalists tried various nominating devices to recoup their sagging fortunes. In 1804 their congressional caucus nominated Pinckney and Rufus King, but they were swamped in the election. In 1808 the Federalists abandoned the congressional caucus and tried a secret delegate convention in New York which some historians have dubbed the first national nominating convention.[12] They held another secret convention in New York in 1812, but by 1816 they had given up making presidential nominations altogether.

As the Republicans advanced from being the dominant party to being the only party, they continued to use their congressional caucus to pick their nominees. In 1804 they were so confident of success that they held a public caucus

[11] Hamilton's strategy failed. All 65 Federalist Electors voted for Adams, but one voted for John Jay instead of Pinckney; so the Federalist electoral vote was: Adams 65, Pinckney 64, Jay 1; Republicans Jefferson and Burr each received 73.

[12] Cf. Samuel Eliot Morrison, "The First National Nominating Convention," *American Historical Review*, 17 (July, 1912), 744-763.

to renominate Jefferson, and in the succeeding three election years they continued the practice. In 1820 everyone knew there would be no Federalist nominee and therefore no contested election. And since President James Monroe, the Republicans' leader and certain nominee, believed that the mischiefs of party competition had at last been cured by the elimination of the Federalists, it would not be appropriate to hold a caucus. So none was held.

CAUCUS TO CONVENTION

1. *Death of the Congressional Caucus,* 1824. We have seen that the congressional caucus nominating system was born as an incident in intraparty factional struggles in 1800. It died in 1824 as a casualty of another factional struggle. After the election of 1820 there was no Federalist party and no chance of a Federalist candidate in 1824. So choosing the Republican nominee would amount to choosing the President. Like Jefferson, Monroe intended to respect the two-term tradition; but, unlike Jefferson, he had not groomed a political heir apparent. So by 1823 at least five serious contenders for the nomination had emerged—John Quincy Adams, John C. Calhoun, Henry Clay, William H. Crawford, and Andrew Jackson—and none of the five had put any great distance between himself and his rivals.

Most of the politicos in all camps recognized that *how* the nomination would be made would do much to determine its outcome. If the party reverted to its traditional congressional caucus system, it looked as though each candidate would get some votes, but Crawford would get the most and, even with only a plurality, would win the nomination and the election. So how people felt about the proper nominating method was correlated very highly indeed with which candidate they supported. The legislature of Crawford's home state of Georgia expressed their support for him *and* declared that the congressional caucus was the only legitimate nominating procedure. The legislature of Jackson's home state of Tennessee formally nominated Jackson and added a resolution condemning the congressional caucus system as unrepresentative and unconstitutional. Henry Clay's home state legislature in Kentucky nominated him, and supporters of all four anti-Crawford candidates held public meetings denouncing "King Caucus" and calling on members of Congress not to attend.[13]

The Crawford faction, now led by Martin Van Buren, nevertheless believed the caucus was their best chance, so eleven pro-Crawford congressmen issued an invitation to all their colleagues to attend a public caucus in the chamber of the House of Representatives on February 14, 1824. When the day arrived, only 66 of the 216 Republican congressmen attended. In a brief session they nominated Crawford for the presidency and Albert Gallatin for the vice presidency.[14] In the subsequent Senate debate referred to earlier, Samuel Smith of Maryland, a Crawford supporter, put his finger on the main source of the attacks on the congressional caucus method:

> May we not, without offence, believe that men are much governed by the consideration of whether the caucus will or will not support their favorite candidate? And must we not believe that those who have heretofore attended caucuses, will find it difficult to assign any other reason for absenting themselves from what they now censure?[15]

[13] David, Goldman, and Bain, *op. cit.*, p. 16; Dallinger. *op. cit.*, pp. 18-20.

[14] For an eyewitness account of the proceedings, see *Niles' Weekly Register*, February 20, 1824, pp. 389-390.

[15] In Benton (ed.), *op. cit.*, Vol. VII, p. 532. For confirmation. cf Senator Smith's analysis, see Van Buren's view in Robert V Remini,

But winning the argument is not, then or now, the same as winning the election: Crawford finished third in the electoral college count with 41 votes to Jackson's 99, Adams' 84, and Clay's 37. Since then no party's congressional caucus has ever nominated a presidential candidate.

2. *Emergence of the National Convention.* In the period from 1825 to 1828 presidential candidates were put forward by a variety of state-based devices: official acts of state legislatures, unofficial declarations by state legislative caucuses and mixed caucuses, and endorsements by state conventions. But no national agency immediately replaced the defunct congressional caucus.[16] This jumble of local systems worked very well for the Jacksonians, who used it to nominate and elect their leader in 1828. But the anti-Jackson faction, now hardening into a separate party calling themselves first "National Republicans" and then "Whigs," decided that the only way they could hope to defeat "King Andrew" in 1832 would be to unite all their forces in one national movement behind one *nationally* selected candidate. For that purpose they needed some kind of national nominating mechanism, and the best one around seemed to be the national delegate convention pioneered by the minor Anti-Masonic party in 1830.[17] They decided to hold their convention in Baltimore, the nearest big city outside the national capital; and, to avoid offending local sensibilities, they designated the National

---

Martin Van Buren and the Making of the Democratic Party (New York: Columbia University Press, 1959), pp. 83-84; and Charles S. Sydnor, "The One-Party Period of American History," *American Historical Review*, 51 (April, 1946), 445.

[16] Dallinger, *op. cit.*, pp. 29-35; and Samuel R. Gammon, Jr., *The Presidential Campaign of 1832* (Baltimore, Md.: Johns Hopkins Press, 1922), pp. 16-29.

[17] See Charles McCarthy, *The Anti-Masonic Party* in the *Annual Report of the American Historical Association, 1902* (Washington, D.C.: Government Printing Office, 1903), Vol. I, pp. 365-574; and Gammon, *op. cit.*, Ch. II.

Republican caucus of the Maryland legislature to issue the call for the convention for December, 1831. The convention met as scheduled, with 167 delegates from 17 states, and nominated Henry Clay.[18]

These proceedings caused the Jacksonians no loss of sleep. But they had other problems to which calling a national convention also seemed the best solution. Jackson and his chief lieutenant, Martin Van Buren, had decided that John C. Calhoun had to be dumped from the ticket and the vice presidency in 1832, but they knew it would not be easy. Calhoun had many supporters in the state legislatures and state parties, and it seemed possible that if the decentralized nominating methods of 1828 were used again they would be saddled with Calhoun for four more years. So the pragmatic Van Buren, who had been one of the chief defenders of the congressional caucus system in 1824, persuaded Jackson that a national nominating convention dominated neither by congressmen nor by state leaders was the solution. The Jacksonian caucus of the New Hampshire legislature was chosen to issue the call for a Democratic Republican convention to meet in Baltimore in May, 1832. The delegates who came balloted only on the vice presidential nomination and chose Van Buren.[19] Thus America's second great party reform was accomplished, not because the principle of nomination by delegate conventions won more adherents than the principle of nomination by legislative caucuses, but largely because the dominant factional interests of 1824 decided that the caucus system made things harder for them, and the dominant factional interests eight years later decided that national conventions would make things easier for them.

[18] See the account in Dallinger, *op. cit.*, pp. 36-40.
[19] Gammon, *op. cit.*, Ch. IV.

3. *Later Conflicts, Interests, and Outcomes.* Since 1832 the national parties have nominated their presidential and vice presidential candidates by national delegate conventions. However, the rules governing the conduct of those conventions have often been hotly disputed, and in most such contests the candidate and factional interests underlying the pronouncements of principle have been both clear and decisive.

For example, prior to the Whig convention of 1839 some leaders, notably Thurlow Weed of New York, decided that Henry Clay, the party's leader and defeated candidate in 1832, was too unpopular with the voters to be elected but so popular with the party's convention delegates that he was likely to be nominated again. So the trick was to keep the convention from choosing him without totally alienating him and his supporters. As Weed dryly commented later, "The organization of the convention and the mode of proceeding occasioned much solicitude among the friends of different candidates."[20] Well it might. Weed's faction persuaded the convention to drop its customary direct balloting procedure and replace it with a complicated indirect system. Each state delegation chose a committee of three, which canvassed the preferences of its own delegates and reported them to the other delegations through their counterpart committees. Each delegation then balloted secretly, and its committee carried the results to a general meeting of all the committees. The general committee added up the results and reported them to the delegations. The delegations then balloted again, this time under the unit rule, and the votes were aggregated by the general committee. If no candidate received a majority, the procedure would be repeated. In this way,

[20] Thurlow Weed, *Autobiography* (Boston: Houghton Mifflin, 1884), Vol. I, p. 481.

the Weed faction hoped, the delegates would be able to vote against Clay secretly and thus avoid any reprisals from his enthusiasts back in their states. It worked perfectly: the general committee announced that William Henry Harrison had received 148 votes to Clay's 90 and was the nominee.[21]

In 1832, the first Democratic National Convention adopted, with Martin Van Buren's strong approval, a rule requiring a two-thirds majority for the nomination. In the 1844 convention this rule cost him the nomination. His majorities on the early ballots were not enough to win, and he was finally passed over for James K. Polk, history's first "dark horse" winner. The convention's rules, which had seemed suitable and just to the Van Buren men in 1832 and in the two subsequent conventions, suddenly struck them as grossly unfair: they issued a statement denouncing the 1844 convention as

the first instance of a body of men, unknown to the laws and the Constitution, assuming to treat the American Presidency as their private property, to be disposed of at their own will and pleasure; and, it may be added, for their own profit.[22]

The legitimacy of the two-thirds rule, it seemed, depended on whose ox it gored.

Many subsequent Democratic and Republican conventions have witnessed credentials fights over the seating of rival delegations from particular states. In most, the debates over the merits of the cases have not concealed the fact that what was really at stake was votes for or against particular candidates.[23] The most recent instance

[21] *Niles' Weekly Register*, December 14, 1839, pp. 248-252.

[22] Quoted in Ostrogorski, *op. cit.*, p. 86.

[23] See, for example, the descriptions of the credentials contests in the Republican conventions of 1912 and 1952 in David, Goldman, and

was certainly no exception. The hottest fight in the 1972 Democratic Convention was over the issue of whether all 271 pro-McGovern delegates chosen in California's winner-take-all primary should be seated or only the 120 delegates that would be proportional to his 44 per cent of the popular vote. Both sides filled the debates in the Credentials Committee and on the convention floor with appeals to democracy, fair play, the spirit of reform, not changing the rules in the middle of the game, and so on. But these lofty principles were not the only stakes. As the New York *Times* told it:

> The formal arguments were heavy with irony. The anti-McGovern lawyers, representing in fact the more conservative branch of the party, argued that the California law violates "the spirit of reform," as exemplified in the same guidelines their committee members had largely been voting down in other challenges.. . . The question was clearly decided on political, not substantive, grounds. . . . Almost no one who supported Mr. McGovern voted for the challenge; almost no one who supported anyone else voted against it.[24]

Both sides also exuded a moral indignation reminiscent of the Van Buren pronouncements in 1844. McGovern denounced the Credentials Committee's decision to split the delegation as "an incredible, cynical, rotten political steal" and hinted that he might not support Humphrey or any other candidate nominated "by crooked and unethical procedures of the kind that were used in this committee room." The anti-McGovern coalition were equally

---

Bain, *op. cit.*, pp. 262-264, 365-366, 381-382.

[24] New York *Times*, June 30, 1972, p. 20. The quotations in the following paragraph are from the same source.

indignant when the Convention Chairman, Lawrence O'Brien, ruled that the 120 California delegates whose credentials had not been challenged would be allowed to vote and that the majority required to win would be only a majority of the delegates qualified at the time of the vote. The indignation of both sides was certainly genuine, but it stemmed mainly from their correct understanding that the outcome of these procedural fights would decide who won the nomination.

George McGovern's own changing views of party reform provide another striking illustration. From 1969 to 1971 he chaired the commission that wrote the party's new delegate-selection rules. Two of their innovations became especially controversial. One was the rule requiring representation on each state's delegation of women, young people, and minority groups "in reasonable relationship to their presence in the population of the State."[25] The other was the rule prohibiting a presidential candidate or any other party leader from determining which individuals would make up any slate of candidates for delegate, whether pledged to a presidential candidate or not.[26]

No one was more enthusiastic about the new rules than McGovern. He praised them repeatedly during his campaign for the 1972 nomination, and often attacked other candidates, especially Edmund Muskie, for trying to get around them. When he won the nomination he declared it was "all the more precious in that it is the gift of the most open political process in our national history."[27] But soon after his disastrous defeat in the November election he expressed a different view. Testifying before the party's new commission on party organization, he declared that

[25] Guidelines A-1 and A-2, in Commission on Party Structure and Delegate Selection, *Mandate for Reform* (Washington, D.C.: Democratic National Committee, 1970), pp. 39-40.

[26] Guideline C-6, in *ibid.*, p. 48.

[27] *Congressional Quarterly Weekly Report*, July 15, 1972, p. 1781.

the quotas for population groups should be dropped, and that presidential candidates and other party leaders should be guaranteed the right "to protect the integrity of the method that chooses delegates in their name." The wire service account added: "Asked why McGovern did not take the views then that he now espouses, an aide said, "We were running for president then."[28]

Does this sort of thing show that McGovern and his opponents were hypocrites, knaves, or fools? I think not. McGovern and his supporters certainly believed he would be a better candidate and President than any of his rivals, and those who supported the other aspirants believed the same of them. Surely one need not be a hypocrite, knave, or fool to believe that rules which make it easier to nominate a good candidate are preferable to those likely to saddle the party and perhaps the nation with a bad one. Speaking more generally, to say that some people advocate some party reforms and oppose others because they believe that changing the rules will help or hurt the candidates and policies they believe in is to say that, in politics as in all other forms of human conflict, the rules make a difference in determining who wins and who loses. Not *all* the difference, but enough to force the prudent to pay them heed.

Of all the rules affecting political parties, the most basic are those which determine their legal status as private associations or public agencies. The course of party reform in America has given our state and local parties a legal position very different from those of the parties in any other Western nation, and in the 1970s our national courts are considering taking the last step down this road. I shall devote the remainder of this chapter to considering the issues, developments, and consequences involved.

[28] Milwaukee *Journal*, April 12, 1973, p. 4.

Putting the Parties in Their Place

PARTIES AS PRIVATE ASSOCIATIONS OR PUBLIC AGENCIES

THE LEGAL STATUS OF PARTIES IN WESTERN DEMOCRACIES

In the United States, as in every other Western democratic polity, political parties were originally created, organized, and operated entirely outside the law. By that I mean that they were established by the voluntary and unofficial acts of private citizens, not by formal acts of public agencies. Thus they were, strictly speaking, neither "in compliance" with the law nor "against" the law; rather they were "unknown to" the law.

As the parties grew in membership and organization, and as their political role became more prominent, in America as elsewhere a number of disputes arose about how the parties should be made to conduct their affairs properly. Some argued that they should be stripped of their private character and subjected to legal regulation; others argued that parties should retain their extralegal status and any necessary reforms should be made by the parties voluntarily changing their own rules.

The result has been a wide range of different legal statuses for the parties among Western nations. The principal variations are these:[29]

No Legal Mention of Parties. At one extreme of the spectrum stand the nations in which parties remain entirely outside the law: e.g., Australia, France, Eire, Finland, Luxembourg, and New Zealand. In these nations no constitutional provision, statute, administrative regulation, or judicial decision mentions parties directly in any way. The candidates' party affiliations do not appear on

[29] Evidently this question has not interested contemporary students of comparative political parties, and I am aware of no comprehensive survey covering it. The typology and data in the text are drawn mainly from studies of parties in various individual nations and from the summaries in Wolfgang Birke, *European Elections by Direct Suffrage* (Leiden: A.W. Sythoff, 1961).

75

election ballots. There is no legal regulation of the parties' internal organizations and operations. To be sure, most of these nations have "corrupt practices" laws prohibiting bribery and intimidation of voters and regulating campaign contributions and expenditures; but they are directed at individual candidates and their organizations, not at parties.

Candidates' Party Affiliations Printed on Official Ballots. The minimum legal recognition of parties is given by those nations—e.g., Denmark, the Netherlands, and Great Britain[30]—which allow or require the party affiliations of parliamentary candidates to be printed on official election ballots, but otherwise have no legal regulation, subsidy, or other recognition of the parties' existence. Sweden has a variation reminiscent of American practice until late in the nineteenth century: there is no official ballot, and the voter may vote for a party's list of candidates by writing its name at the top of a piece of paper and depositing it in the ballot box, or by depositing a list of names printed by a party and given to the voter.[31]

Exclusion of Nonparty Candidates. In Austria and Italy only the names of the parties, and the voter cannot vote no "independent" candidates are allowed. The same result is obtained in Israel by the fact that the ballot contains only the names of the parties, and the voter cannot vote for individual candidates at all.

[30] And in Britain only very recently and tentatively, with the 1969 amendment to the Representation of the People Act which allows each parliamentary candidate to have on the ballot under his name a description of up to six words, including, if he wishes, the political party nominating him: *Halsbury's Statutes of England* (3d ed., London: Butterworth's, 1969), Vol. XI, Parliamentary Elections Rules, Schedule II, Rules 7 and 14. The Labour Government initially proposed a requirement that each candidate's party label be printed on the ballot and that the constituency's returning officer be empowered to decide disputes over which person is entitled to a particular label. They later dropped this proposal for the much milder version adopted.

[31] Birke, *op. cit.*, p. 52.

Putting the Parties in Their Place

Optional Legal Regulation of Internal Party Affairs. Norway's Nomination Act of 1921 sets forth an *optional* model procedure for the selection of any party's parliamentary candidates under which the candidates from each of the twenty multimember constituencies or "provinces" are chosen by a convention composed of delegates elected by the party's enrolled members in the province's various communes. If a party chooses to use this procedure, the national government will pay the expenses of its provincial conventions. If it chooses not to—and the major parties in the predominantly urban provinces of Bergen and Oslo usually do choose not to—then they are free to use other nominating methods, though in that case they receive no public subsidy.[32]

Mandatory Legal Regulation of Internal Party Affairs. Other than the United States, the only Western nation with mandatory legal regulation of its parties' internal affairs is the Federal Republic of Germany.[33] Article 21 of the 1949 Basic Law gives the parties constitutional status and outlaws parties that seek the overthrow of the democratic system of government. The Electoral Law of 1956 provides that half (258) of the members of the Bundestag shall be elected from single-member constituencies and that the party affiliation of each candidate shall be

[32] Henry Valen and Daniel Katz, *Political Parties in Norway* (Oslo: Universitetsforlaget, 1964), pp. 21-22; and Valen, "The Recruitment of Parliamentary Nominees in Norway," *Scandinavian Political Studies* (New York: Columbia University Press, 1966), pp. 121-166, esp. p. 122.

[33] The account in the text is pieced together from Lewis J. Edinger, *Politics in Germany* (Boston: Little, Brown, 1968), Ch. VIII; Arnold J. Heidenheimer, "Federalism and the Party System: The Case of West Germany," *American Political Science Review*, 52 (September, 1958), 809-828; Gerhard Loewenberg, "Parliamentarism in Western Germany," *American Political Science Review*, 55 (January, 1961), 87-102; and Uwe W. Kitzinger, *German Electoral Politics* (Oxford: Clarendon Press, 1960).

printed on the official ballot. The other half are elected by a party list system of proportional representation from the various *Länder*, and the lists come mainly from parties with at least five members in an outgoing *Land* or Federal parliament. A party with fewer M.P.s or a new party can get its list on the ballot only by filing a petition signed by a specified number of voters and certifying that the party has a written constitution, a written program, and a "democratically elected management committee."

Moreover, the 1956 law stipulates the procedures by which both old and new parties must choose their parliamentary candidates: they must be chosen in the constituencies by direct secret vote of the enrolled members of the party, or in a nominating convention of delegates chosen by the members. If the party's management committee for the *Land* objects to the list so chosen, a second vote must be held, and its results are final. Finally, the Germans go the Americans one better by providing that every party whose organization conforms to "democratic principles" in this manner is entitled to a public subsidy of its campaign expenses.

But West Germany has had these rules only since 1956, and most other Western nations, as we have seen, have few comparable laws or none at all. In the legal regulation of internal party affairs the United States still stands alone, as it has ever since the late nineteenth century when the states first began to enact their elaborate regulatory codes.

LEGAL REGULATION OF AMERICAN STATE AND LOCAL PARTIES

From their origins in the 1790s until after the Civil War, American political parties at all levels were, as V.O. Key put it, "entirely private association[s]; it was no more illegal to commit fraud in the party caucus or primary than it would be to do so in the election of officers of a drinking club."[34] Aside from corrupt practices laws regulating campaigns, the first American statutes directly and explicitly regulating the internal affairs of parties were adopted by California and New York in 1866. The California law was comprehensive but optional: it required advance public notice of party meetings selecting party officers of candidates for public office, and it laid down qualifications for the right to participate; but the statute applied only if a party so requested. The New York law was mandatory but limited: it applied to all parties without their request, but merely prohibited bribery or intimidation in the conduct of party caucuses and conventions. Other states followed suit in the 1870s and early 1880s, producing a melange of statutes—some limited, some general, some mandatory, some optional—regulating the conduct .of party affairs.[35]

The conversion of the state and local parties from private associations to public agencies came mainly in the 1890s and early 1900s as a result of the states' widespread adoption of the partisan version of the Australian ballot. This was and is a system in which general-election ballots are marked in secret, printed, distributed and counted entirely by public authorities, but have each candidate's partisan affiliation printed next to his name. Massachusetts adopted the nonpartisan Australian ballot in 1888,

[34] V.O. Key, Jr., *Politics, Parties & Pressure Groups* (5th ed., New York: Thomas Y. Crowell, 1964), p. 375.

[35] The most useful historical accounts include: Charles E. Merriam, *Primary Elections* (Chicago: University of Chicago Press, 1908), pp. 9-62; Howard R. Penniman, *Sait's American Parties and Elections* (4th ed., New York: Appleton-Century-Crofts, 1948), pp. 193-194, 616-619; and Allen F. Lovejoy, *La Follette and the Establishment of the Direct Primary in Wisconsin, 1890-1904* (New Haven, Conn.: Yale University Press, 1941), pp. 31-43. The most comprehensive survey, now outdated in only a few minor respects, is Joseph R. Starr, "The Legal Status of American Political Parties," *American Political Science Review*, 34 (June, August, 1940), 439-455, 685-699.

and a year later Indiana adopted the partisan system. By 1892 another thirty-one states had gone to the new system, and most chose Indiana's partisan variant.

Robert M. La Follette and the other Progressive leaders then pushed hard for the legal regulation of parties, contending that the general adoption of the partisan Australian ballot provided both the need and the justification for such regulation. They argued that, if the parties were allowed to continue operating outside the law, they would continue in their accustomed ways of boss-rule, corruption, and fraud. Now the remedy was at hand. As Richard Hofstadter sums up their view:

> First the citizen must reclaim the power that he himself had abdicated, refashioning where necessary the instruments of government. Then—since the Yankee found the solution to everything in laws—he must see that the proper remediable laws be passed and that existing laws be enforced.[36]

From the mid-1890s on, state after state was conquered by the forces contending that statutory regulation of parties is a logical and necessary extension of the principles underlying the Australian ballot. Since a party label appears next to each candidate's name on the ballot, it was said, it is necessary to be sure who is legally entitled to it. Since the parties are benefited by having the ballots say which candidates belong to which parties, they must accept the regulations necessary to ensure proper conduct of their affairs. Of the many expressions of this prevailing Progressive view, perhaps the best known was that set forth in La Follette's gubernatorial message to the Wisconsin legislature in 1903:

[36] Richard Hofstadter, *The Age of Reform* (New York: Vintage Books, 1955). p. 202.

Putting the Parties in Their Place

Every established practice and custom which tends to impair in any degree the citizens' right of suffrage subverts the principles of representative government and undermines the foundations of democracy. . . . There are important proceedings, vitally essential to the right of suffrage, which are foundational, not only to manhood suffrage, but to the whole structure of government itself. What transpires back of the moment when the voter receives his official ballot must be as strongly fortified and as sacredly guarded as that which follows the consummation of this right after he receives the official ballot. . . . If by bad practice and bad laws all the proceedings which control in the making of the ballot to be voted are taken out of the hands of the voter, his right of suffrage is not only impaired, but he has been deprived of it.[37]

The Progressives' arguments—and formidable political clout—won the day. By 1920 most states had adopted a succession of mandatory statutes regulating every major aspect of the parties' structures and operations.[38] First came laws requiring the use of secret ballots in all intraparty elections of officers and candidates. Next came laws laying down the qualifications for party membership by stipulating who could participate in intraparty elections. These were followed by statutes specifying the number, powers, and composition of party committees and conventions. And the climax of the Progressive reforms arrived when most states adopted Wisconsin's great contribution to the art of governance—the direct primary.

It should be emphasized again that almost all of these laws are *state* laws, regulating only state and local parties.

[37] In Ellen Torelle (ed.), *The Political Philosophy of Robert M. La Follette as Revealed in His Speeches and Writings* (Madison, Wis.: Robert M. La Follette Company, 1920), pp. 73-74.

[38] The successive waves of legislation are described in Merriam, *op. cit.*, pp. 32-42.

Curing the Mischiefs of Faction

Congress undoubtedly has the constitutional power to pass comparable laws governing the national parties' conventions and committees, but it has never done so, and up to now the federal courts have had little to say about their constitutional status. Consequently, America's *national* parties are at present almost as private and "unknown to the law" as their counterparts in other Western nations.[39] But their privacy is now under challenge as never before, and I shall conclude this chapter by reviewing the issues and stakes involved in that challenge.

CURRENT CONFLICT OVER THE LEGAL STATUS
OF THE NATIONAL PARTIES

1. *Primacy of National Party Rules v. Primacy of State Primary Laws.* In 1908 the state of Oregon adopted the first law requiring the selection of delegates to national party conventions by direct primaries rather than by state party conventions or committees.[40] By 1973, presidential primary laws were in force in twenty-three states and the District of Columbia. Altogether primaries chose or bound nearly 70 percent of the delegates to both parties' conventions.

From the beginning, presidential primaries have created the anomaly that delegates to national, extralegal conventions are selected according to the different laws of different states. Inevitably this has occasionally raised the question of what would happen if a state's delegation is selected in accordance with that state's laws but in violation of the national party's rules. The first answer

[39] Cf. "One Man, One Vote and Selection of Delegates to National Nominating Conventions," *The University of Chicago Law Review*, 37 (1969-70), 542-545; and David, Goldman, and Bain, *op. cit.*, p. 3.

[40] For accounts of the adoption and, in some cases, repeal of presidential primaries prior to the 1970s, see James W. Davis, *Presidential Primaries: Road to the White House* (New York: Thomas Y. Crowell, 1967), pp. 24-37, and Louise Overacker, *The Presidential Primary* (New York: Macmillan, 1926).

came in the Republican convention of 1912, the first in which any delegates had been chosen by direct primaries. In the California primary two Taft delegates won in a San Francisco district even though theTheodore Roosevelt slate won a plurality in the state as a whole and thus won, under California law, the entire state delegation. The Taft delegates demanded their seats, and the convention had to decide whether its own rules prohibiting the unit rule and requiring selection of delegates by districts were superior to California's election laws. The Taft forces had the votes, and they seated the San Francisco two on the declared ground that the convention was the final judge of its delegates' credentials. But four years later, in their less contentious convention of 1916, the Republicans adopted a resolution declaring that "all delegates from any State may be chosen from the State-at-large *or* part from the Congressional Districts, in conformity with the laws of the State in which the election occurs."[41]

In the 1960s the Democrats reasserted the superiority of the national party's rules over state laws. The 1960 convention added each state's national committeeman and committeewoman to its delegation without regard to state laws. The 1964 convention adopted a rule that in selecting its delegates each state party must assure "that voters in the State, regardless of race, color, creed, or national origin, will have the opportunity to participate fully in Party affairs." In 1968 the convention refused to seat the entire "regular" delegation from Mississippi on the ground that they had violated this party rule even though they admittedly had been selected in full accordance with Mississippi law.[42] In 1969 the McGovern-Fraser commis-

[41] Quoted in David, Goldman, and Bain, *op. cit.*, p. 196, emphasis added. See also Charles E. Merriam and Louise Overacker, *Primary Elections* (Chicago: University of Chicago Press, 1928), pp. 186-187.

[42] *The Presidential Nominating Conventions of 1968* (Washington, D.C.: Congressional Quarterly Service, 1968), pp. 97-98.

sion stopped just short of a frontal challenge to California's winner-take-all presidential primary law by "urging" rather than "requiring" each state party to provide for the "fair representation of minority views on presidential candidates."[43] For reasons we reviewed earlier, the 1972 convention refused to unseat any of the legally elected pro-McGovern delegates even though the slate received only 44 percent of the popular vote; but the convention did unseat the equally legally elected 59 Daley delegates from Cook County because the procedures by which they had been slated violated the party's rules. These were the first instances since 1912 in which any delegates elected by direct primaries were seriously challenged, let alone unseated.[44]

Although the fact was little noticed by the press at the time, the 1972 Democratic convention adopted a number of new rules strongly asserting the supremacy of the national party over state laws. One requires that in 1976 all delegates shall be "chosen in a manner which fairly reflects the division of preferences expressed by those who participate in the Presidential nominating process in each state. . . ," which presumably commits the party not to accept all the delegates from any future winner-take-all primary. A second provides that:

> the voters of [a] delegation shall ... be recorded as polled without regard to any state law, [state] Party rule, resolution or instruction binding the delegation or any member thereof to vote as a unit with others

[43] Guideline B-6 in *Mandate for Reform*, p. 44.

[44] Cf. David, Goldman, and Bain, *op. cit.*, pp. 264-265; and Overacker, *op. cit.*, pp. 166-168. In late 1973 an Illinois appellate court held that the State's direct primary laws supersede any conflicting national party rules, including the McGovern-Fraser guidelines: "Once elected, any question of the delegates' qualifications to hold office is beyond the authority of party functionaries; it is a legal right properly protected by the courts": *Wigoda v. Cousins* (1973), 42 LW 2183, at 2184.

or to cast his vote for or against any candidate or proposition.[45]

In other words, the national Democratic party's rules now provide that, if a delegate is required by the primary laws of his state to vote for a particular candidate but he chooses to vote for another, the convention will honor his choice and not enforce the state's laws. A third new rule prohibits the selection of delegates by direct primaries in which persons other than Democrats are allowed to vote—a direct challenge to the "open" primaries of Wisconsin and Michigan.[46]

In short, the present legal status of the national parties may be summarized thus. No one denies that Congress has as much power to regulate the national party conventions and committees as the state legislatures have to regulate their state and local counterparts. But Congress has not used its powers, and they are not likely to be used in the near future. The position currently taken by the dominant forces in both national parties is that, in the absence of congressional legislation to the contrary, the national parties are private associations, not public agencies; and as such they have a right to govern their own affairs by their own rules without regard to contrary provisions in state laws.

However, the power of the national parties to live by their own rules is now facing another, and far more threatening, attack. A number of state and national party factions are challenging various national party rules in the federal courts. Their basic view is that, congressional legislation or not, the national parties play a major role in the presidential selection process and are thus public

[45] Report of the Rules Committee of the 1972 Democratic National Convention, June 27, 1972 (mimeo.), Chapter VI, section C, paragraph 3.

[46] *Congressional Quarterly Weekly Report*, July 15, 1972, p. 1777.

agencies which must govern their affairs in accordance with the Federal Constitution. To date, the leading court challenges have been the following.

2. *Court Challenges to the National Parties' Private Status.* In 1971 the Democratic National Committee adopted a new rule providing that delegates to the national conventions would henceforth be apportioned among the state parties on a formula of 53 percent for the states' strengths in the Electoral College and 47 percent for the states' average vote for the Democratic presidential candidates over the three preceding elections.[47] Shortly thereafter two suits challenging the constitutionality of the formula were brought in the Federal District Court for the District of Columbia. The first was *Georgia v. National Democratic Party*, in which the Attorney General of Georgia argued that the apportionment formulae of both parties were unconstitutional because they violated the one-man-one-vote principle laid down by the Supreme Court in the succession of legislative apportionment cases stemming from *Baker v. Carr* (1962). The only constitutionally valid formula, Georgia claimed, was one based exclusively on the states' populations. The district court ruled against this claim, and the Court of Appeals for the District of Columbia sustained the decision, for reasons we shall review in a moment.

The second case was *Bode v. National Democratic Party*, in which the Center for Political Reform and the Americans for Democratic Action challenged the Democrats' apportionment formula on different grounds. The plaintiffs agreed with the Georgia argument that the formula is a proper matter for the courts to review, but they contended that only the principle of one-*Democrat*-one-vote satisfies the Court's standards. To the surprise

[47] *Congressional Quarterly Weekly Report*, February 19, 1971, pp. 417-418.

of many, Judge June L. Green upheld their claim and ordered the party to reallocate its convention delegates exclusively on the basis of past presidential votes. The DNC appealed, and the Court of Appeals overruled her decision.

In deciding these two cases the courts tackled a question basic to the whole legal status of the parties: do the national parties' convention apportionment rules constitute "state action" sufficiently to require that they conform to the same apportionment standards demanded for Congress and the state legislatures? The D.C. Court of Appeals in both cases answered with a strong "Yes!" They admitted that "the issue is not without difficulty, where, as here, the activity allegedly violative of the Constitution has been historically viewed as a purely private political matter." But they concluded that this can no longer be the case:

> As is the case with regard to the election of members of Congress, the major parties' nomination procedures play such an important role in the presidential selection process that they can hardly be said not to be "integrally related" to the subsequent general election. The electorate's choice in the general election is effectively restricted to the nominees of the two parties. By placing the nominees' names on the ballot, the states, in effect, have adopted this narrowing process as a necessary adjunct of their election procedures. Therefore, every step in the nominating process —especially the crucial determination of how many delegates each state party is to be allotted—is as much a product of state action as if the states themselves were collectively to conduct such preliminary conventions.[48]

[48] *Georgia v. National Democratic Party*, 447, F. 2d 1271 (1971) at 1276. The point was reaffirmed in the CPR-ADA case: "There is no

Curing the Mischiefs of Faction

The Supreme Court did not rule on either of the two delegate apportionment cases, so the Court of Appeals' decisions gave only the second highest legal sanction to the proposition that the national parties are public agencies. But in its midnight consideration of the California and Illinois credentials challenges in July, 1972, the Supreme Court faced the question without—for the time being—deciding it.

The facts were these. The Credentials Committee of the Democratic National Convention in late June voted, by 71 to 61, not to seat the 59 delegates from Cook County. They gave two reasons. First, while the Cook County delegates had been elected in accordance with the Illinois primary law, there had not been open access to the process by which the winning delegate slate had been drawn up, and this was a violation of the McGovern-Fraser commission's Guideline C-6. Second, Cook County party officials had endorsed and worked for the official slate; this was a violation of Guideline C-5.[49] The Cook County group challenged the Committee's action in the District of Columbia district court, and Judge George L. Hart, Jr. (who had been the Republican chairman for the District of Columbia) held Guideline C-5 unconstitutional and ordered the 59 delegates seated.[50] The Democratic National Committee appealed to the D.C. Court of Appeals, which considered the case together with the California challenge.

---

doubt that the allocation among the States of delegates to a national party convention is subject to the equal protection requirements of the Fourteenth Amendment": *Bode v. National Democratic Party*, 452 F. 2d 1302 (1971) at 1305. In both cases, however, the Court of Appeals held that the DNC's 53-47 apportionment formula was acceptable under the Constitution. For a more detailed discussion, see Judith H. Parris, *The Convention Problem* (Washington, D.C.: Brookings Institution, 1972), pp. 18-21.

[49] The texts of the two Guidelines are in *Mandate for Reform*, pp. 47-48.

[50] New York *Times*, June 20, 1972, pp. 1, 25.

The California challenge, as we have seen, involved a clash between California's winner-take-all primary law and the McGovern-Fraser commission's *recommendation* in Guideline B-6 that "each State party. . .adopt procedures which will provide fair representation of minority views on presidential candidates."[51] In the June primary McGovern's slate won 44 percent of the popular vote to 39 percent for the Humphrey slate, but under California law the entire McGovern slate was elected. On June 29 the Credentials Committee voted, by 72 to 66, to seat only 120 of the McGovern delegates and to distribute the remaining seats among the other candidates' slates in proportion to their shares of the popular vote in the primary. The McGovern forces challenged this decision in the federal courts, and on July 5 the D.C. Court of Appeals ruled unanimously to uphold the Committee in the Illinois case, but voted by 2 to 1 to overrule it in the California case. According to Frank Mankiewicz, McGovern's campaign director, this decision meant that, if the Convention subsequently were even to consider upholding the Credentials Committee or entertain any other parliamentary maneuver that would raise the possibility of denying seats to any of McGovern's delegates, it would constitute contempt of court. Whether his view was pure principle, pure candidate partisanship, or a mixture of both, it was surely as strong an assertion of the public-agency theory of the national parties as we have had from any party leader since La Follette.[52]

The Democratic National Committee appealed the California decision to the Supreme Court, arguing that the national party is a private association and hence, both as a matter of constitutional law and a matter of public policy, it should have the power to regulate its own internal

[51] *Mandate for Reform*, p. 44.
[52] New York *Times*, July 6, 1972, pp. 1, 28.

affairs without judicial interference.[53] In an unusual special evening session on July 7 the Supreme Court voted, by 6 to 3, to stay the execution of the Court of Appeals' order and thereby barred judicial interference with the Credentials Committee's actions in both the Illinois and California cases. The Court's majority declined to rule on the merits of either case, but declared that there was not enough time before the convention opened on July 10 to hear arguments and make an authoritative ruling, and so the issue would have to be left up to the party's machinery. But the *per curiam* opinion gives some clues as to how the majority viewed the basic issues:

> no holding of this Court up to now gives support for judicial intervention in the circumstances presented here, involving as they do relationships of great delicacy and essentially political in nature. . . . Judicial intervention in this area traditionally has been approached with great caution and restraint. . . . It has been understood since our national political parties first came into being as voluntary associations of individuals that the convention itself is the proper forum for determining intra-party disputes as to which delegates shall be seated. . . . In light of the availability of the convention as a forum to review the recommendations of the Credentials Committee, . . . the lack of precedent to support the extraordinary relief granted by the Court of Appeals, and *the large public interest in allowing the political processes to function free from judicial supervision*, we conclude the judgments of the Court of Appeals must be stayed.[54]

[53] New York *Times*, July 5, 1972, p. 30; *ibid.*, July 6, 1972, p. 37.
[54] *O'Brien v. Brown*, 409 U.S. 1 (1972) at 4-5, emphasis added.

But this was not the only way the issues could be viewed. Mr. Justice Thurgood Marshall's dissent suggests another way that might have been followed in 1972 and may yet be followed in future cases:

> the action of the Party in these cases was governmental action, and therefore subject to the requirements of due process. The primary election was, by state law, the first step in a process designed to select a Democratic candidate for President. . . . In these circumstances, the primary must be regarded as an integral part of the general election. . . and the rules that regulate the primary must be held to the standards of elementary due process.[55]

The politics, if not the law, of the matter was settled by the convention. The McGovern forces had the votes, and the convention voted by 1,618.28 to 1,238.22 to seat all 271 McGovern delegates from California. They also voted, by 1,486.05 to 1,371.55, *not* to seat the 59 delegates from Cook County.[56] This settled the disputed 210 convention votes, which after all were the main concern of most of the litigants. But the decisions of the McGovern and Daley forces to carry their factional quarrels outside the party and into the courts set in train a series of events that are likely to culminate, sometime in the 1970s, in a final and authoritative decision by the Supreme Court on the question of whether the national parties shall remain private associations or become, like their state and local affiliates, public agencies whose internal rules and procedures are subject to judicial supervision. It is not my task to advise the Court how to rule on the issue or to speculate about how it is likely to rule. But it seems appropriate to consider some of the leading issues involved.

[55] *Ibid.*, at 12-13.
[56] *Congressional Quarterly Weekly Report*, July 15, 1972, p. 1723.

Curing the Mischiefs of Faction

1. *The Constitutional Issue.* As we observed earlier, there is no legal question but that state legislatures have the constitutional power to regulate state and local parties' internal affairs, and that Congress has a comparable power to regulate the national parties. The constitutional issue has been whether, in the *absence* of such legislation, the state and federal courts should nevertheless treat the parties as public agencies whose rules and decisions are all subject to judicial oversight.

Up to the early 1940s, neither the federal nor state courts took a clear or consistent stand on this issue. Some judges argued that the parties were purely private associations and should remain so. For example, a minority opinion of the New York State Supreme Court in the early 1900s contended that

> The right of electors to organize and associate themselves for the purpose of choosing public officers is as absolute and beyond legislative control as their right to associate for business or social intercourse or recreation. The legislature may, doubtless, forbid fraud, corruption, intimidation or other crime in political organizations the same as in business associations, but beyond this it may not go. . . . An alliance cannot be made by one person alone. It requires the action of several whose rights are equal; no one can ally himself with others solely by his volition. Therefore [we] do not see that an elector has greater rights to join a party, unless on the conditions that the party prescribes, than he has to insist upon entering a partnership or contributing his quota of capital, against the wish of the parties then conducting the business. . . .[57]

[57] *People v. Democratic Committee*, 164 N.Y. 335, quoted in Floyd R. Mechem, "Constitutional Limitations of Primary Election Legisla-

But historically this has been a losing argument. Since the early 1940s the federal courts have increasingly taken the position that the right to vote in a state primary election—and therefore the right to participate in performing a state party's most important function, the choosing of its candidates—is protected by the Fourteenth and Fifteenth Amendments just as much as the right to vote in general elections. In *U.S. v. Classic* (1941) the Supreme Court held that, where state law makes the primary election "an integral part of the procedure of choice" of U.S. Representatives, "or where in fact the primary effectively controls the choice, the right of the elector to have his ballot counted at the primary. . .is protected just as is the right to vote at the [general] election."[58] In *Smith v. Allwright* (1944) the Supreme Court employed this doctrine to declare unconstitutional a rule of the Texas Democratic party excluding Negroes from voting in its primaries, thereby ending the venerable Southern institution of the "white primary."[59]

Since the Smith case, the Supreme Court has made no decisions on the status of parties, but various federal district courts and courts of appeal have made a number of relevant rulings, including the 1972 decisions just reviewed. The strongest assertion of the public agency position yet made by a federal court was handed down by the Court of Appeals for the Fourth Circuit in *Rice v.*

---

tion," *Publications of the Michigan Political Science Association* (March, 1905), 141. Joseph Starr observes that prior to the adoption of state regulatory laws, the parties' right to select candidates, determine their own memberships, and manage their own affairs was generally held to be part of their "inherent powers" incident to the constitutional right of freedom of association. However, the state laws have by now almost entirely superseded the parties' "inherent powers": Starr, *op. cit.*, pp. 447-451. See also Merriam, *Primary Elections*, pp. 101-102.

[58] *U.S. v. Classic*, 313 U.S. 299 (1941), at 318.
[59] *Smith v. Allwright*, 321 U.S. 649 (1944).

Elmore (1947). The case arose from South Carolina's effort to evade the consequences of the Smith decision by repealing all laws even mentioning parties or primaries, hoping thereby to establish the parties as purely private associations with the power to exclude anyone they wished. The South Carolina Democratic party promptly used that power to exclude Negroes from its affairs, but all was for naught. The Court of Appeals ruled that the party was still de facto an agent of the state and thus its exclusion of Negroes violated the Fourteenth and Fifteenth Amendments. More significantly, the Court added:

> The fundamental error in [South Carolina's] position consists in the premise that a political party is a mere private aggregation of individuals, like a country club, and that the primary is a mere piece of party machinery. The party may, indeed, have been a mere private aggregation of individuals in the early days of the Republic, but with the passage of the years, political parties have become in effect state institutions through which sovereign power is exercised by the people.[60]

Whether the Supreme Court takes this view will determine whether the national parties will lose their traditional status as private associations. But what status *should* the parties have? For most of us, that is the significant question, and it seems to me that the answer depends mainly on how one stands on other, more fundamental, policy issues.

2. *The Secrecy and Legitimacy Issues.* It has been said that Americans are the most law-*respecting* people in the world, though not the most law-*abiding*. Certainly one of the most enduring and powerful elements in our national

[60] *Rice v. Elmore*, 165 F. 2d 387 (1947), at 389.

creed is the vision inherited from the Founding Fathers of "a government of laws and not of men." Felix Frankfurter put it this way:

> Fragile as reason is and limited as law is as the institutionalized medium of reason, that's all we have standing between us and the tyranny of mere will and the cruelty of unbridled, undisciplined feeling.[61]

In this view there seem to be two alternatives. One is a kind of lawless Hobbesian state of nature, with each man out to get his and let the devil take the hindmost, and where the only arbiter is *force majeure*. The other is a kind of Platonic paradise, where each man seeks his own good through pursuing the general good, and decisions are made only in accordance with right reason and the eternal principles of justice embodied in law.

Many Americans have drawn from this government-of-laws view the corollary that in public life only that which is specifically legal is legitimate, and that to be outside the law is little better than to be against the law. If an organization operates outside the law, it usually operates in secret; the only reason for secrecy is to conceal ignoble purposes and illegitimate behavior; so secret covenants secretly arrived at are *in themselves* evidence of conspiracy against the common good.[62]

American parties have always struggled to survive in an atmosphere colored by this view. Their roots lay in

[61] *Felix Frankfurter Reminisces* (New York: Reynal, 1960), p. 19.

[62] A typical early expression of this longstanding view was made by Senator John Holmes of Maine in the March, 1824 debate over the congressional caucus:

> when the Representatives act with open doors, and expose their views and motives to the world, the people's rights are safe; the danger lies in secret combinations, in compacts to divide and distract—in private meetings to prevent public meetings. It is here that bargains may be made, and management and intrigue to be practised with success.

In Benton (ed.), *op. cit.*, Vol. VII, p 523.

the secret revolutionary societies formed to overthrow British rule.[63] After independence they became more public and open, but for many Americans then and now they have never lost their reputations as facades erected by devious men to mask secret conspiracies for selfish purposes. For example, to Washington and many other Federalists the surest evidence of the subversive nature of the Jeffersonian Democratic Societies was the fact that they met in secret.[64] Much the same notion contributed to the replacement of the legislative caucus with the delegate convention in the 1820s and 1830s. The Anti-Masonic party pioneered the national convention, and the movement for which it spoke denounced not only the Freemasons but *all* secret societies and secret meetings.[65] One of the main arguments in the Progressives' case for the legal regulation of parties was the charge that boss rule and corruption were direct and inevitable consequences of the manipulation of caucuses and conventions by wirepullers making secret deals in smokefilled rooms. Hence the only way to end the corruption was to force the parties' decision making into the open by imposing direct primaries and the legal regulation of party organization.[66]

The antisecrecy leitmotiv appeared again in the McGovern-Fraser commission's condemnation of "secret caucuses, closed slate-making. . .and a host of other procedural irregularities." Its proposals to end these evils included requiring adequate public notice of party meetings, limiting to 10 percent the proportion of delegates that could be chosen by state committees, and insisting that all party members be guaranteed a "full and meaningful opportu-

---

[63] Dallinger, *op. cit.*, pp. 7-12.

[64] Luetscher, *op. cit.*, pp. 60-62; Hofstadter, *The Idea of a Party System*, p. 95.

[65] Lee Benson, *The Concept of Jacksonian Democracy* (New York: Atheneum, 1964), pp. 17-20; McCarthy, *op. cit.*, pp. 544-549.

[66] Hofstadter, *The Age of Reform*, pp. 70-72.

nity to participate" in the processes by which slates of delegates pledged to particular candidates were put together.[67] But the commission, unlike many earlier reformers, took the position that the best way to make the Democratic party truly open, public and nonconspiratorial is to allow it to reform and enforce its own rules, not to chain it with Acts of Congress and court rulings. As a member of the commission, I can testify that, while only a few of us made this argument explicit, the commission's whole approach to making the national conventions more open and representative was premised upon the view that, whatever may be the law of the matter, it is good *policy* for the nation to preserve the private status which the national parties have traditionally enjoyed.

3. *The Policy Issue.* Since the parties' legal status became a salient issue in the late nineteenth century, some commentators have taken a similar view. Herbert Croly, for example, had less faith than most of his Progressive associates in the proposition that the best way to cure a political evil is to pass a law against it. Often, he said, the practical effect is merely to substitute one evil for another. This was, he felt, particularly true of the Progressives' efforts to legally force upon the parties democratic structures and procedures. Even if these efforts were successful, the effect would be to alter the parties' essential character and thus their ability to perform the functions for which they were created. In Croly's words:

A party is essentially a voluntary association for the promotion of certain common political and economic objects. It presupposes a substantial agreement of opinion and interest among the members of the party, and a sufficient amount of mutual confidence.

[67] *Mandate for Reform*, p. 11, and Guidelines C-1, C-5, and C-6, pp. 45-48.

If they differ vitally in interest and opinion, and have little or no confidence in one another, the association should not be regulated; it should to that extent be dissolved. By regulating it and by forcing it to select its leaders in a certain way, the state is sacrificing the valuable substance of partisan loyalty and allegiance to the mere mechanism of partisan association. Direct primaries will necessarily undermine partisan discipline and loyalty. They will make it more necessary for every voter to belong nominally to either one of the two dominant parties; but the increasing importance of a formal allegiance will be accompanied by diminishing community of spirit and purpose. Such is the absurd and contradictory result of legalizing and regularizing a system of partisan government.[68]

Others have since enlarged on Croly's theme. Schattschneider, for instance, argued that the parties should control the decisions of public authorities by forcing them to operate as a responsible team rather than as independent entrepreneurs; but their ability to do so depends largely upon preserving their extralegal character so that they can offset the fragmentation and dispersion of power built into the legal order.[69] And it is interesting to note the discussion stirred in Great Britain in the late 1960s by the proposal that the parties be legally recognized by printing candidates' party affiliations on ballots and empowering public officials to decide who is legally entitled to each party's label. The distinguished British scholar of parties and elections, David Butler, argued that, once

[68] Herbert Croly, *Progressive Democracy* (New York: Macmillan, 1915), pp. 342-343. For a similar view, see William MacDonald, *A New Constitution for a New America* (New York: B.W. Huebsch, 1921), pp. 141-142.

[69] E.E. Schattschneider, *Party Government* (New York: Farrar and Rinehart, 1942), pp. 11-12.

the ownership of the party label was made a matter for government to decide, the parties would find it much harder to deal themselves with their internal schisms and conflicts.[70]

Butler's argument might well be pondered by Americans. In both countries the essence of conflict resolution by the courts is the public confrontation of adversaries ending in victory for the plaintiff or defendant. It is important to remember that many litigants and their attorneys try to settle their disputes "out of court" by private negotiations and agreements *before* the confrontation takes place. Evidently, and understandably, they regard a trial as many diplomats regard war—not the ideal way to settle a dispute but a last resort when all others have failed.

Until recently, American parties, when left to themselves, have typically resolved their conflicts "out of court" by similar private negotiations among competitors, ending in some kind of accommodation all concerned feel they can live with. But American state and local parties have not been left to themselves for nearly a century now, and our national parties may soon lose what remains of their power to settle their own disputes.

If they do, much of the responsibility will have to be borne by the factional leaders in both parties who have sought victories in the courts they could not win in their parties' forums. We have already noted the court challenges brought since 1970 by Democratic factions of both

[70] David Butler, letter to the London *Times*, November 27, 1968, p. 11. The British journalist R.L. Leonard added the argument, which may sound strange to American ears, that "the necessity of obtaining legal judgments [about who owns a party label] would make party affairs justiciable, and might lead, e.g., to would-be candidates going to law about allegedly improper selection procedures": *Elections in Britain* (London: D. Van Nostrand, 1968), fn 8, p. 128. The Government, as noted in footnote 30 above, eventually dropped this proposal for a much weaker one.

right and left against party decisions on convention apportionment, delegate selection rules, and the seating of delegates. In addition, the Ripon Society has challenged the Republicans' new convention apportionment rule.[71] And when, in late 1973, the Democratic National Committee's counsel held that all old or new delegate-selection rules would have to be approved by the DNC, the chairperson of the new Delegate Selection Commission declared "quite possibly we'll go to court."[72] If the parties' factional leaders continue to regard winning particular disputes as more important than keeping them out of the courts, we can hardly expect the Supreme Court to preserve the national parties' privacy much longer.

Whatever may be the disposition of the constitutional issue, the policy issue of putting parties in their proper place ultimately turns upon the questions of what functions we want them to perform in our society and what internal organization and legal status we calculate are most likely to encourage them to behave as we wish. These questions will be our main concern in the next chapter.

[71] *Congressional Quarterly Weekly Report*, September 16, 1972, p. 2339.

[72] *Congressional Quarterly Weekly Report*, September 29, 1973, p. 2575.

CHAPTER FOUR

Making the Parties Behave

In the demonology of some America-watchers, the 1968 Democratic National Convention has joined the My Lai massacre and the Watergate break-in as among the most disgraceful episodes in the nation's history. Some have paid less heed to what the delegates did inside the International Amphitheater than to what Mayor Daley's police did in the streets outside; even so, the convention's composition, procedures and outcome were denounced as never before.[1] The party's McGovern-Fraser reform commission appointed in 1969 declared that in the selection of the 1968 delegates "meaningful participation of Democratic voters was often difficult or costly, sometimes completely illusory, and, in not a few instances, impossible."[2]

The bill of particulars included several items. More than a third of the delegates had been selected prior to 1968,

[1] For example, a widely read account by three British journalists labeled the process by which Humphrey won the nomination as "the survival of the unfittest," the nomination itself as "a throne of bayonets," and the whole affair as "the reign of piety and iron": Lewis Chester, Godfrey Hodgson, and Bruce Page, *An American Melodrama: The Presidential Campaign of 1968* (New York: Dell, 1969), esp. "Act" X.

[2] Commission on Party Structure and Delegate Selection, *Mandate for Reform* (Washington, D.C.: Democratic National Committee, 1970), p. 10.

"before either the major issues or the possible presidential candidates were known." Even in 1968 "secret caucuses, closed slate-making, widespread proxy voting—and a host of other procedural irregularities—were all too common." Less than half of the delegates were chosen or bound by direct primaries. And the result was a highly unrepresentative convention: only 5 percent of the delegates were black compared to 11 percent of the general population; only 13 percent were women, compared to 51 percent of the population; and only 4 percent were "young people" (that is, people between the ages of eighteen and thirty), compared to 27 percent of the population.[3]

The 1972 convention was the most reformed in history, thanks in good part to the McGovern-Fraser commission's guidelines. Under the new rules access to the delegate-selection process was wide open. Far more people participated than ever before in the preliminary precinct, county, and state conventions. Seven states had newly adopted presidential primaries, and over two-thirds of the national delegates were elected or bound by them. There were few secret caucuses, little closed slate-making, and no proxy voting. Of the delegates selected under the reformed rules, 13 percent were black, 40 percent were women, and 21 percent were between eighteen and thirty. And to cap it all, the convention's presidential nominee began his acceptance speech by avowing, "My nomination is all the more precious in that it is the gift of the most open political process in our national history."[4]

There was one other great contrast between the reformed and unreformed conventions. It is shown in Table 4. The 1968 nominee's performance in the November general election was the second best for a loser in this

[3] *Ibid.*, pp. 10-11.
[4] *Congressional Quarterly Weekly Report*, July 15, 1972, p. 1781.

TABLE 4
EPILOGUE TO TWO CONVENTIONS

	Popular Votes	Percent of Two-Party Popular Votes	Number of States Carried	Electoral votes	Percent of Two-Party Electoral Votes
Nominee of unreformed convention, 1968	31,275,166	49.6	14	191	38.8
Nominee of reformed convention, 1972	29,170,383	38.2	2	17	3.1

Sources: 1968 returns from Richard M. Scammon (ed.), *American Votes, 1968* (Washington, D.C.: Governmental Affairs Institute-Congressional Quarterly, 1970), p. 1. 1972 returns from *Congressional Quarterly Weekly Report,* March 10, 1973, pp. 531–539.

century. The 1972 nominee's performance was the third worst for a loser in history—despite the fact that the Democratic party lost only a few seats in the House of Representatives and actually increased its Senate seats, governorships, and control of state legislatures.

Can we say, then, that the new rules and the new-style convention were the sole or main reason for the 1972 disaster? Some Democrats believe so: The 1973 manifesto by the newly formed Coalition for a Democratic Majority declared:

> We believe that in repudiating the Democratic/"New Politics" presidential candidacy in this election while re-electing a Democratic Congress, the voters were speaking with precision and sophistication. What they said was that American society should continue on in that very Democratic tradition which, abandoned by the forces temporarily in control of the national Democratic Party in 1972, was usurped in some measure by the Republicans.[5]

[5] Published as an advertisement in the Washington *Post*, February 14, 1973, italics removed.

103

Other Democrats deny these allegations. They argue that it is difficult to defeat an incumbent President even under the most ideal conditions and that the size of the Nixon landslide in 1972 was largely the product of his campaign organization's unlimited funds and unscrupulous use of espionage and sabotage.

Political science has no way of determining precisely what proportion of the explanation for the relative size of the Humphrey and McGovern defeats should be assigned to the new delegate-selection rules and the new-style convention. But from at least one point of view the question is irrelevant: if we believe that the prime object of a party convention is to represent, say, some biological characteristics of the party members, then we should judge conventions only by how accurately their delegates reflect the party members' traits. If, however, we believe that the convention's prime object is to put the party in the best possible position to win the ensuing election, then quite another kind of criterion is in order; for, as Henry Jones Ford drily observed in 1898, "there appears to be no connection between the extent to which a constituent quality has been imparted to a convention, and the force with which its decisions appeal to public confidence and support."[6]

This chapter is concerned with how the advocates and opponents of party reform, past and present, have wanted the parties to behave and how they have calculated the parties could be made to behave properly. We shall see that many of the conflicts over this issue have turned, in the end, upon this same question of whether the party's highest goal and ultimate criterion should be representativeness or success at the polls.

[6] *The Rise and Growth of American Politics* (New York: Macmillan, 1898), p. 296.

MAKING THE PARTIES REPRESENTATIVE

THE DEMAND FOR REPRESENTATIVENESS

We observed in the first chapter that American political parties were initially organized in the 1790s, not to make political organization more representative or more democratic, but to win elections. Madison and Jefferson sought to block Hamilton's programs by replacing his followers in Congress and the executive with their own, and Hamilton was forced to defend his policies by the same means. Both sides pursued their partisan goals mainly by forming organizations to "concert their strength," as they put it: that is, by designating candidates for elective offices and rallying support behind them.

In Chapter 3 we saw that the earliest party reforms were intended to make parties more representative of their supporters. For the nomination of candidates for statewide offices, the legislative caucuses replaced mass meetings in the capital cities—mainly to better represent, it was said, the party faithful living in other areas. The legislative caucuses then generally gave way to "mixed" caucuses to better represent party members in districts with no party legislators. And in the 1820s and 1830s delegate conventions replaced the legislative and congressional caucuses because they were thought to be even more representative since they sprang directly from the party rank-and-file. A typical expression of this view appeared in the call by friends of Henry Clay for a nominating convention to be held in Kentucky in 1830 for the purpose of putting his name forward for the presidency:

Issuing directly from the people, [this convention] will hear and proclaim their genuine sentiments. Essentially popular in its character and composition, it will command respect and secure confidence by its plain straightforward movement, without intrigue, without the corrupt agency of caucus management, without any other motive of origin but the spontaneous impulse of the people themselves.[7]

But the conventions never satisfied everyone as being ideally representative. For example, the national party conventions often disputed the proper apportionment of their delegates among the state parties, an issue which is, of course, entirely one of representativeness. The state conventions generally used the same apportionment rules as those for the lower houses of their legislatures, with the counties electing delegates in numbers proportional to their populations.[8] But the national government was a federation of states, and the organizers of the early national conventions felt they had to take this into account. Thus the first national convention, called by the Anti-Masonic party for 1830, allotted to each state delegation the same number of votes its state had in the Electoral College rather than apportioning them entirely on the basis of population.[9] The rule seemed sensible to most major-party politicians as well, and was adopted by the National Republicans in 1831 and the Democratic Republicans in 1832.[10]

[7] Quoted in James Staton Chase, "Jacksonian Democracy and the Rise of the Nominating Convention," *Mid-America: An Historical Review*, 45 (October, 1963), 233. See also Edgar E. Robinson, *The Evolution of American Political Parties* (New York: Harcourt, 1924), p. 102; and Richard P. McCormick, *The Second American Party System* (Chapel Hill, N.C.: University of North Carolina Press, 1966), p. 349.

[8] Chase, *op. cit.*, pp. 244-245.

[9] Charles McCarthy, *The Anti-Masonic Party: A Study of Political Anti-Masonry in the United States, 1827-1840*, published in the *Annual Report of the American Historical Association, 1902* (Washington, D.C.: Government Printing Office, 1903), Vol. I, pp. 365-574, *passim*.

[10] Paul T. David, Ralph M. Goldman, and Richard C. Bain, *The Politics of National Party Conventions* (Washington, D.C.: Brookings

However, the delegate-*selection* procedures for the first conventions were, at least by McGovern-Fraser standards, a bit casual. For example, the Democratic party of Tennessee sent no delegates whatever to the 1835 national convention in Baltimore, and yet the state's entire fifteen votes were cast by one Edward Rucker. This evidently raised some eyebrows back home, for Rucker later explained himself in a letter to the Nashville *Union*:

Sir: You will discover my name introduced into the proceedings of the Baltimore convention. To prevent all misunderstanding, I make the following statement. I was not delegated to act in that convention. I happened to be in Baltimore at the time of its sitting, and after the delegates from the different states had their credentials examined by the committees appointed for that purpose, there appeared to be no one present representing Tennessee. This circumstance seemed to be deeply regretted by many, and upon its being mentioned that I was there, and a Tennesseean, it was suggested by some that I might vote, which I accordingly did.[11]

However the delegates may be selected, a number of political scientists have charged that there are far too many of them. No body of two or three thousand, they say, can be a truly deliberative or even orderly assembly. Much of the conventions' disorder, hoopla, and Roman

---

Institution, 1960), xp, 164-165, See also Frederick W. Dallinger, *Nominations for Elective Office in the United States* (New York: Longmans, Green, 1897), pp. 36-40.

[11] *Niles' Weekly Register*, Vol 48, June 20, 1835, p. 273. A later commentator, however, cleared up some of the mystery by noting that "Rucker, it should be observed, belonged to the Van Buren faction, which controlled the convention": Howard R. Penniman, *Sait's American Parties and Elections* (4th ed., New York: Appleton-Century-Crofts, 1948), p. 278, fn. 28.

circus atmosphere which so offend our sensibilities are consequences of their Brobdingnagian size. So a reform often urged by academics is to reduce the number of delegates to a total—perhaps 500 or so—which will enable the convention to be as deliberative and decorous as, say, a faculty meeting.[12]

But politicians more than political scientists must live with the consequences of size, and they have put other values ahead of decorum and deliberation. From the 1830s to the 1970s they have often increased but never reduced the number of delegates. This has stemmed in part from the eagerness of party supporters to attend conventions, and of party leaders to keep them happy. But it has also been a response to demands to make the conventions more representative. The point was put forcefully in a letter to the O'Hara commission by Donald O. Peterson, one of the founders of the reformist New Democratic Coalition established in 1968:

> A smaller convention would undoubtedly become a group of party elitists with little or no grass roots representation. A convention that restricts representation will not serve our party well in the future.[13]

Peterson's argument has always appealed to those who value representation above decorum and deliberation. It was never more powerful than in 1972. The McGovern-Fraser commission's Guidelines A-1 and A-2 required each state's delegation to include representation of minority groups, women, and young persons "in reasonable relationship to their presence in the population of the state."[14]

[12] Two of the more extended expositions of the criticism are: Judith H. Parris, *The Convention Problem* (Washington, D.C.: Brookings Institution, 1972), pp. 86-96; and David, Goldman, and Bain, *op. cit.*, pp. 213-217.

[13] Quoted in Parris, *op. cit.*, p. 92.

[14] *Mandate for Reform*, p. 40.

Making the Parties Behave

We shall consider later the clash of theories of representation out of which this reform emerged, but its practice is our concern here. A number of state parties originally chose their delegations in compliance with the other guidelines, but then saw that they contained too many middle-aged WASP males and dangerously few women, young people, and members of minority groups. Some parties asked some of the WASP males to step aside, but others received permission to enlarge their delegations and fill the extra slots with members of the underrepresented groups. They could not, of course, get extra *votes*, so the increased number of delegates had to cast fractional votes. The Republicans have never allowed fractional voting, but the Democrats have been allowing more delegates than votes and the use of fractional votes ever since 1852. In 1972, however, their arithmetic became more complex than ever. For example, the final vote on the motion to seat the entire California delegation was 1,618.28 Yes to 1,238.22 No. It included such delegation counts as: Wyoming, 4.4 to 6.6; New Hampshire, 9.9 to 8.1; Georgia, 21.75 to 31.25; and—in a stirring tribute to representativeness—Maryland, 27.83 to 25.17![15]

However, up to 1972 the main device used to make delegate apportionment more representative had been the "bonus vote." It is intended to make the delegations' shares of the convention's voting strength more nearly represent their state's relative contributions to the party's electoral success than is possible with the electoral-vote or straight-population formulae. It is accomplished by awarding extra or "bonus" votes to states and congressional districts in which the party's candidates for Congress, President, or

[15] *Congressional Quarterly Weekly Report*, July 15, 1972, p. 1723. For the pressures for increased size and fractional voting, see Parris, *op. cit.*, pp. 86-92.

governor have won or exceeded a minimum number of votes. It was pioneered by the Republicans in 1916 as a result of their convention debacle in 1912—which also took place in Chicago, by the way. That year's bitter contest for the nomination between William Howard Taft and Theodore Roosevelt was settled by the fact that the eleven southern delegations went solidly for Taft; these delegations had 23 percent of the convention's votes, even though in the election of 1908 they had contributed less than 7 percent of the party's popular votes and none of its electoral votes. The Roosevelt forces charged that their leader had been cheated of the nomination by this "travesty of representation"; they walked out, formed a third party, split the Republican vote in November, and thereby elected the Democrat. Fearful of another such disaster, the Republican National Committee proposed, and the 1916 convention adopted, a rule providing an extra convention vote for each congressional district in which 7,500 Republican votes had been cast for President in 1908 or for Congressman in 1914.[16]

The Republicans' bonus-vote rule was subsequently changed several times, and the Democrats adopted their own version in 1940. Its underlying party-vote idea was applied even more directly in 1972. The Democrats, as we noted in Chapter 3, adopted a new rule apportioning delegates according to a formula of 53 percent for the states' strengths in the electoral college and 47 percent for the states' average votes for the Democratic presidential candidate in the three preceding elections. The Republicans revised their apportionment rules in a way that will increase the total number of delegates by over

---

[16] David, Goldman, and Bain, *op. cit.*, pp. 166-168. See also George H. Mayer, *The Republican Party, 1854-1964* (New York: Oxford University Press, 1964), Chs. VIII-IX.

a third in 1976.[17] We also observed that the apportionment formulae of both parties have been challenged in the federal courts. Some challengers argue that allocating votes according to population is the only principle acceptable under the Federal Constitution. Others contend that only allocation according to party voting strength is acceptable. However the Supreme Court ultimately decides this issue, the fact that members of both parties have challenged the established rules signals the most recent appearance of one of the oldest dilemmas in party reform. Many reformers in all epochs have believed that party organization should, above all else, be truly representative. But they have never agreed, and still do not agree, on just *who* should be represented and how.

THE CONFLICT OVER REPRESENTATION

Most students of political philosophy and political science are painfully aware of how complex is the theoretical problem of what constitutes true representation and how difficult is the organizational problem of how to achieve it. Hanna Pitkin's brilliant exploration of the concept sets forth in sharp focus the many theoretical dilemmas, but their solutions seem a good deal more blurred to my eyes, and perhaps to hers as well.[18] For example, is the essence of representation the fact that the constituents have *authorized* the representative to act in

[17] *Congressional Quarterly Weekly Report*, August 26, 1972, pp. 2119-2120. The problem is thoroughly discussed in Parris, *op. cit.*, Ch. 2.

[18] Hanna Fenichel Pitkin, *The Concept of Representation* (Berkeley, Los Angeles and London: University of California Press, 1967). I have also found useful: Hanna Fenichel Pitkin (ed.). *Representation* (New York: Atherton Press, 1969); J. Roland Pennock and John W. Chapmen (eds.), *Representation* (New York: Atherton Press, 1968); and Alfred de Grazia, *Public and Republic: Political Representation in America* (New York: Alfred A. Knopf, 1951).

their place? Or that he is *accountable* to them? Or that he shares their class or religion or race? Or that he acts in their best interest? Or what?

I do not wish to poach on Professor Pitkin's territory, and so I shall not reveal the final and correct answers to these questions. But as a member of the McGovern-Fraser commission, I can testify with conviction that conflicting theories of representation were the wellsprings both of the commission's greatest internal disagreements and of the principal difficulties our guidelines created for the Democratic party.[19]

To begin with, most of the commission's twenty-eight members believed in what I shall call preferential proportional representation. That is, we believed that each state delegation should include supporters of the various candidates in the same proportions as they exist among the state's Democrats—though, as we shall see in Chapter 5, we were far from agreed on just who *is* a party member and therefore entitled to representation. Accordingly, we drew up a number of guidelines intended to guarantee to every party member full and free access to all procedures for selecting delegates. And we declared, in our Guideline B-6, that

> The Commission believes that a full and meaningful opportunity to participate in the delegate selection process is precluded unless the presidential preference of each Democrat is fairly represented at all levels of the process. Therefore, the Commission urges each State Party to adopt procedures which will provide fair representation of minority views on presidential candidates and recommends that the 1972 Convention

[19] This section draws heavily from my paper "The Line of the Peas: The Impact of the McGovern-Fraser Commission's Reforms," (presented at the 68th Annual Meeting of the American Political Science Association, Washington, D.C., September 8, 1972).

adopt a rule requiring State Parties to provide for the representation of minority views to the highest level of the nominating process.[20]

When we had settled that question, however, we plunged into our hottest dispute over the issue of whether we should add another, and quite different principle of representation. About half the commissioners also insisted on what I shall call "proportional *demographic* representation." This is one of several versions of what Professor Pitkin calls "descriptive representation." In political philosophy it is the doctrine that a representative body should be a sample, a miniature, a map-to-scale of the population it represents and should therefore include in its ranks members of the population's main groups in about the same proportions as they exist in the population.[21] The commissioners who took this view singled out three groups —women, young people, and minority ethnic groups—as the prime victims of the gross overrepresentation (as they saw it) of middle-aged WASP males in 1968 and before. Like some other advocates of descriptive representation, they argued, in effect, that the interests and views of women are best represented by women delegates, those of blacks by black delegates, and so on. So they pressed for some kind of quota system requiring that each state's delegation include women, young people, and members of minority groups "in reasonable relationship to the group's presence in the population of the State."[22]

The other commissioners (eventually including me; but see Chapter 6) opposed any such quotas. We based our arguments mainly on what Professor Pitkin calls the "authorization" and "accountability" theories of repre-

[20] *Mandate for Reform*, p. 44.
[21] See Pitkin, *The Concept of Representation*, Ch. 4.
[22] Guidelines A-1 and A-2, *Mandate for Reform*, p. 40.

sentation[23]—though not even the two professorial commissioners dared use such abstract language. We contended that requiring representation of biological characteristics was at odds with the commission's other objectives of open access and representation of preferences. The party could provide for a fair fight or it could provide for a guaranteed result, we said, but it could not provide for both.

In the end the commission voted, by 10 to 9, to require representation of women, young people, and members of minority groups. Many people have asked since, why only *those* groups? Why not also guaranteed representation for, say, people over sixty-five, or labor union members, or poor people? The answer is simple, if not edifying: the commissioners who believed in descriptive representation spoke only for the special interests of women, youth, and minority ethnic groups; and those of us who sought a different kind of representation did not counter by pressing for the special interests of other groups.

The data on the demographic composition of the 1972 convention cited earlier show that the quota system produced the results its proponents sought. Some commentators have charged that this victory for the quota system played a major role in the party's 1972 electoral disaster, and there is little doubt that its future status will be a major issue in party circles for some time to come.[24]

However, the dispute about the right kind of party organization has never been exclusively a clash about what *kind* of representation should be the parties' prime goal. From the beginning the doctrine that representativeness is the highest ideal has been challenged from two very different points of view, each of which has had its triumphs. One holds that no matter how you tinker with the compo-

[23] Pitkin, *The Concept of Representation*, Ch. 3.

[24] See, for example, the antiquotas statement by the Coalition for a Democratic Majority: *Congressional Quarterly Weekly Report*, December 2, 1972, pp. 3097-3098.

sition and conduct of caucuses and conventions they can never become faithful transmitters of the party members' will; accordingly, they must be superseded by institutions establishing direct, unmediated rule by the rank-and-file. The other view holds that a party should never go all out for representativeness or direct democracy or any other abstract general principle, but should choose whatever organization and procedures will put it in the best possible position to win elections. We shall consider each view in turn.

ACHIEVING DIRECT RULE BY PARTY MEMBERS

PARTICIPATORY DEMOCRACY AND THE ATTACK ON REPRESENTATION

1. *In Political Theory.* Since modern theories of democracy first began to appear in the mid-seventeenth century, a succession of political philosophers has argued that only direct and unmediated popular rule is true democracy. Representation in any form is inherently antithetical to popular rule, and it can never be more than a barely acceptable alternative to out-and-out tyranny.

The fountainhead of this view, described by one of his modern followers as "the theorist *par excellence* of participation,"[25] was Jean Jacques Rousseau. One of the two main arguments against the legitimacy of representation appears in this passage in *The Social Contract*:

> Sovereignty cannot be represented for the same reason that it cannot be alienated; its essence is the general will, and that will must speak for itself, or it does not exist; it is either itself or not itself: there is no intermediate possibility. The deputies of the

[25] Carole Pateman, *Participation and Democratic Theory* (Cambridge: at the University Press, 1970), p. 22.

people, therefore, are not and cannot be their representatives; they can only be their commissioners, and as such are not qualified to conclude anything definitively. No act of theirs can be a law, unless it has been ratified by the people in person; and without that ratification nothing is a law.[26]

Rousseau's successors elaborated this argument by contending that it is not possible for one person's ideas to pass through the mind of another without emerging distorted. Anyone who has ever graded a set of examination papers will find it hard to dispute this judgment, though some may not derive from it all of the corollaries derived by Rousseau and his school.

The other great argument against representation and for direct democracy is the doctrine that the full development of every human being's potential is the prime object of government and that this object can be achieved only if the people directly and actively participate in making their own political decisions.[27]

In recent years participatory democracy has become one of the most prominent elements in the creeds of many theorists and movements protesting the values and structures of such Western institutions as universities, governments, and businesses. Tom Hayden, Frantz Fanon, and Paul Goodman are some of the writers who come to mind, and one thinks of such movements as the Students for a Democratic Society and other "New Left" student rebel-

---

[26] Jean Jacques Rousseau, *The Social Contract*, translated from the French by Charles Frankel (New York: Hafner, 1947), Book III, Chap. XV, p. 85. For Rousseau's views on how to minimize the evils of representation in a full-scale nation-state, see his *The Government of Poland*, translated from the French by Willmoore Kendall (Indianapolis, Ind.: Bobbs-Merrill, 1972), esp. Ch. VII, pp. 35-37.

[27] This argument is particularly stressed by Pateman, *op. cit.* See also Peter Bachrach, *The Theory of Democratic Elitism: A Critique* (Boston: Little, Brown, 1967).

lions in various universities around the world.[28] But these prophets and their followers and chroniclers seem unaware of the fact that the participatory-democracy view has been heard longer and with greater impact in the area of party reform than in any other area of American life. The story is worth telling in some detail.

2. *In Conflict over Party Reform.* In Chapter 2 we observed that, from the nation's beginnings until well after the Civil War, many eminent Americans condemned political parties, however organized, on the ground that their whole reason for being is to interfere with the fundamental right of the sovereign people to freely choose their elected officials. In their view "party reform" is a waste of time, since the parties are bound to do damage no matter how they are structured. Thus a typical Federalist pamphlet of 1806 denounced the Republicans' nominating caucus in Baltimore in these flavorsome phrases:

A diminutive faction, and ambitious as the disciples of a Catiline or a Bonaparte, in a few wards of our city, aspiring to engulph in its rapacious maw all the rights of the whole People, and assuming powers above both law and constitution, has presumed to deliberate for you, to elect for you, and to Dictate to you whom you shall have as Representatives in the ensuing Legislature! . . .What! Shall twenty anonymous men, self appointed. . .have the arrogance to exercise with success the rights of 30,000 Freemen, and thus disfranchise them of those liberties which they have sworn not to relinquish but with their heart's blood? It cannot be true.[29]

[28] A useful analysis and anthology is Terence E. Cook and Patrick M. Morgan, *Participatory Democracy* (San Francisco: Canfield Press, 1971).

[29] Quoted in George D. Luetscher, "Early Political Machinery in the United States" (Philadelphia: University of Pennsylvania Ph.D. Thesis, 1903), pp. 105-106; for a similar Federalist condemnation of the Republicans' state legislative caucus in New Hampshire, see p. 123.

The Federalists had no monopoly on this view (or on pungent rhetoric). Hezekiah Niles, a good Republican, said in an 1824 editorial about his party's congressional caucus:

> "As my soul liveth" I would rather learn that the halls of Congress were converted into common brothels than that the caucuses of the description stated should be held in them. I would rather that the sovereignty of the States should be re-transferred to England, than that the people should be bound to submit to the dictates of such an assemblage. But the people will not succumb to office-hunters. . . . The great mass of the American people feel that they are able to judge for themselves; they do not want a master to direct them how they shall vote.[30]

Niles and others of his persuasion had more success than Tom Hayden or Paul Goodman have had, at least up to now. The state and national legislative caucuses were driven out of the nominating process and replaced by delegate conventions said to be more representative of the parties' ordinary members. But some commentators detested the conventions as much as the caucuses, and for the same reasons. Thus an 1835 editorial in the Nashville *Banner* said of the new national conventions:

> So long as we live and breathe American air, we will resist the insidious proposition (whencesoever and wheresoever it may originate), to lay at the feet of village politicians and placemen [i.e., party hacks seeking patronage jobs], who most usually fill *conventions*, the inestimable privilege of thinking and acting for ourselves in the choice of our rulers.[31]

[30] Quoted in M.I. Ostrogorski, "The Rise and Fall of the Nominating Caucus, Legislative and Congressional," *American Historical Review*, 5 (December, 1899), 272-273.

[31] Quoted in *Niles' Weekly Register*, Vol. 48, March 15, 1835, italics in the original.

Making the Parties Behave

The most powerful attack on the parties' state delegate conventions was mounted by the Progressive movement from 1890 to 1920, and it achieved their general replacement by the direct primary. Richard Hofstadter's insightful study of the movement points out that its ideal was a society in which the free individual forms his judgments and elects his public officials without being organized or herded about by party bosses or committees or conventions or any other kind of intermediary. Hofstadter continues:

> At the core of their conception of politics was a figure quite as old-fashioned as the figure of the little competitive entrepreneur who represented the most commonly accepted economic ideal. This old-fashioned character was the Man of Good Will, the same innocent, bewildered, bespectacled, and mustached figure we see in the cartoons today labeled John Q. Public—a white collar or small business voter-taxpayer with perhaps a modest home in the suburbs. . . . In years past he had been careless about his civic responsibilities, but now he was rising in righteous wrath and asserting himself. He was at last ready to address himself seriously to the business of government. The problem was to devise such governmental machinery as would empower him to rule.[32]

Robert Wood's analysis of the theories underlying the nonpartisan local politics so cherished by the Progressives makes the point from another angle:

> Finally, and most fundamentally, no-party politics implies some positive assumptions about political behavior that go beyond simple antagonism to partisanship. Inescapably, there is a belief that the individual

[32] Richard Hofstadter, *The Age of Reform* (New York: Vintage Books, 1955), pp. 260-261.

can and should arrive at his political convictions
untutored and unruled; and an expectation that in
the formal process of election and decision making
a consensus will emerge through the process of right
reason and by the higher call to the common good.
. . .the citizen, on his own, knows best. . . .[33]

In general, then, the Progressives admired independent
individuals and feared large organizations, whether business corporations or political conventions. Only when such
power was broken could democracy flourish in America.
And since such great power could be broken only by the
greater power of the state, the first step on the long road
must be to reform the government so that it would once
again become the servant of the people rather than the
lackey of the bosses and the trusts. This step could not
be taken by relying entirely on the reform of representative
institutions; the best hope was to build new governmental
machinery to enable the people to bypass all interme-
diaries and rule directly. The initiative, referendum, and
recall; the direct election of U.S. Senators; the short
ballot; women's suffrage; nonpartisan local elections—
these reforms were pressed hard and successfully by the
Progressives, all to the end of enabling the people to rule
directly.[34]
But the Progressives recognized that even these first
steps could be taken only by elected legislators and executives. Since these officials were nominated by political
parties in boss-controlled party conventions, everything

[33] Robert Wood, *Suburbia: Its People and Their Politics* (Boston:
Houghton Mifflin, 1958), p. 157.
[34] Some leading summaries of the Progressive reforms and their
rationales are: Walter E. Weyl, *The New Democracy* (New York:
Macmillan, 1915); Benjamin Parke DeWitt, *The Progressive Movement* (New York: Macmillan, 1915); and Charles E. Merriam, "Nominating Systems," *Annals of the American Academy of Political and
Social Science*, 106 (March, 1923), 1-10.

else depended upon breaking the bosses' power over party nominations. So the absolute top priority among all the reforms on the Progressives' long list was the direct primary. And its purpose, let us be clear, was not to make the parties' conventions more representative but to replace them with direct democracy.[35]

THE BASIC REFORM: THE DIRECT PRIMARY

1. *Development.* In 1842 the local parties in Crawford County, Pennsylvania began selecting their candidates through secret ballots of the party members rather than through delegate conventions. The practice was followed by parties in a few other localities as well but, at most, it was to the modern direct primary what an individual's pledge to give up drinking was to the Eighteenth Amendment.[36] Strictly speaking, a direct primary is a system in which political parties are required by law to choose their candidates through state-administered elections in which any legally qualified person must be allowed to vote.

The general adoption of the direct primary by the states from the early 1900s onward is, in my opinion, the most radical of all the party reforms adopted in the whole course of American history. Though many people worked for it in many states, the earliest and most influential of them all was unquestionably Robert M. La Follette. The story of his role can be briefly told. As we saw in Chapter 2, young La Follette lost the Republican gubernatorial no-

[35] For statements of the top priority of the direct primary in the Progressives' program, see Lincoln Steffens, *The Struggle for Self-Government* (New York: McClure, Phillips, 1906), p. 102; DeWitt, *op. cit.*, pp. 21-22; and La Follette's message to the Wisconsin legislature in 1901 in Ellen Torelle (ed.), *The Political Philosophy of Robert M. La Follette as Revealed in His Speeches and Writings* (Madison, Wis.: Robert M. La Follette Co., 1920), pp. 39-40.

[36] Ernst C. Meyers, *Nominating Systems: Direct Primaries versus Conventions in the United States* (Madison, Wis.: published by the author, 1902), pp. 146-150.

mination in the Wisconsin state convention of August, 1896, because the party's bosses preferred a more docile candidate. La Follette testified quite frankly in his *Auto-biography* that this made him resolve to destroy boss rule at its very roots, and he soon found the way. Shortly after his defeat he learned of several versions of the voluntary "Crawford County system" and of the laws of some states, particularly Kentucky, providing for state supervision of local party nominations if the parties so requested. He added the key idea that such supervision should be both mandatory and complete, and set about promoting the new reform. He was invited to deliver a speech on "The Menace of the Political Machine" at the University of Chicago in February, 1897, and he chose the occasion to make the first of a long series of speeches advocating the mandatory direct primary as the precondition for all other reforms. He pressed his case with redoubled vigor after the 1898 state convention again passed him over. In 1900 he finally managed to win the nomination and the office, and in his first message to the legislature in 1901 he gave the adoption of the direct primary the top priority in his program. The legislature gave him only a watered-down version, which he vetoed. The climax came in 1903 when a more amenable legislature adopted the nation's (and the world's) first mandatory and comprehensive direct primary law.[37]

Radical or not, the reform spread rapidly. Oregon followed suit in 1904, and five more states in 1905. By 1917, forty-four of the forty-eight states had primary laws of

[37] The best short account is Herbert F. Margulies, *The Decline of the Progressive Movement in Wisconsin, 1890-1920* (Madison, Wis.: The State Historical Society of Wisconsin, 1968), pp. 32-71. Also useful is Allen F. Lovejoy, *La Follette and the Establishment of the Direct Primary in Wisconsin, 1890-1904* (New Haven, Conn.: Yale University Press, 1941); and La Follette's own account is revealing: *La Follette's Autobiography* (Madison, Wis.: Robert M. La Follette Co., 1913), esp. pp. 196-198.

some kind, and in thirty-two the laws were, like Wisconsin's, comprehensive and mandatory.[38]

In our own time the direct primary is even more widespread. Thirty-six states now require it for major-party nominations for all statewide offices and for most local offices as well. Three southern states make it compulsory for the Democrats but optional for the Republicans. Nine states have one or another combination of state conventions and primaries. Two states require it for only some statewide offices, and even there nominations for most local offices are made by direct primaries.[39]

The direct primary remains almost exclusively an American institution. Occasionally some parties in other Western nations decide on their own to choose parliamentary candidates by secret votes of the local party members, but no law forces them to do so.[40] Only in West Germany, as we saw in Chapter 3, does the law require that parliamentary candidates be chosen either by the direct secret vote of the parties' enrolled members or in *Land* nominating conventions whose delegates are chosen by similar votes. Occasionally one reads of an English editorial or a Danish politician suggesting their national politics would be improved by adopting the direct primary, but no movements have been launched—or are likely to be launched—to get the necessary laws passed.

So the direct primary remains a uniquely American Way, the fruit of our most radical party reform. But what

[38] Charles E. Merriam and Louise Overacker, *Primary Elections* (Chicago: University of Chicago Press, 1928), pp. 61-66.

[39] *The Book of the States, 1972-1973* (Lexington, Ky.: Council of State Governments, 1972), table on p. 29.

[40] For examples of such "primaries" in Great Britain, see Austin Ranney, *Pathways to Parliament* (Madison, Wis.: University of Wisconsin Press, 1965), pp. 62-65; for similar episodes in Belguim, see Jeffrey Obler, "The Role of National Party Leaders in the Selection of Parliamentary Candidates: The Belgian Case," *Comparative Politics*, 5 (January, 1973), 157-184.

difference has it made for our parties and our political system? It is a question we can hardly evade.

2. *The Original Hopes and Fears.* La Follette and his fellow Progressives expected great things from the direct primary.[41] First, it would end boss rule once and for all. They reasoned that, while it is not difficult to bribe or intimidate a few hundred convention delegates, it is impossible to suborn thousands of voters. Second, it would increase voting turnout and otherwise revive the people's interest in politics by giving them the final say at *every* stage of the electoral process. Third, it would improve the quality of candidates, because no one would have to sell out to a boss to win a nomination. Fourth and most important, it would guarantee the direct and therefore undistorted expression of the people's will. La Follette had a vision of a great future under its benign influence:

> No longer. . .will there stand between the voter and the official a political machine with a complicated system of caucuses and conventions, by the easy manipulation of which it thwarts the will of the voter and rules official conduct. . . . If the voter is competent to cast his ballot at the general election for the official of his choice, he is equally competent to vote directly at the primary election for the nomination of the candidates of his party. . . . Inspired with confidence by the great reformation accomplished in our general elections through the Australian ballot, we advance the standard of reform and demand the application of the same method in making the nomination together with the sovereign right that each citizen shall for himself exercise his choice by direct vote, without

[41] See the list of anticipated benefits claimed by La Follette in his 1903 message to the legislature, in Torelle (ed.), *op. cit.*, pp. 37-39.

the intervention or interference of any political agency.[42]

La Follette also believed that the direct primary would strengthen the parties by purifying them. Other Progressives expected quite a different impact and were glad. The great Nebraska maverick, George W. Norris, spoke for them when he conceded that direct primaries would weaken party control and responsibility. But this alleged evil, he said

I frankly offer as one of the best reasons for its retention. The direct primary will lower party responsibility. In its stead it establishes individual responsibility. It does lessen allegiance to party and increase individual independence, both as to the public official and as to the private citizen. It takes away the power of the party leader or boss and places the responsibility for control upon the individual. It lessens party spirit and decreases partisanship. These are some of the reasons why the primary should be retained and extended.[43]

Most opponents of the direct primary agreed with Norris's empirical analysis, but rejected his evaluation. They argued that the new system would fatally weaken a party's responsibility by taking away its control over its most precious possession, the right to bear its label; the control of that right would now pass from people with a real commitment to the party into the hands of casual

[43] George W. Norris, "Why I Believe in the Direct Primary," *Annals of the American Academy of Political and Social Science*, 106 (March, 1923), 23.

[42] Speech accepting nomination for governor, August 8, 1900, in *ibid.*, pp. 36-37.

passers-by. It would make impossible the careful construction of the "balanced tickets" so necessary to electoral success and to moderating conflict among ethnic groups. It would greatly increase the expense of running for office and thereby favor aspirants with personal fortunes and aspirants financed by special interest groups who would expect something in return. It would make American elections a jumble of squabbles among publicized personalities and fringe movements. It would, in short, remove most of the structure and meaning from politics and thereby bewilder and alienate the people beyond repair.[44]

3. *The Results.* Direct primaries have now been the predominant nominating method in America for well over half a century, and there is surely no lack of data for analyzing their actual behavior as a basis for evaluating their impact and desirability. But, for reasons I do not understand, for every ten scholarly studies of general elections there is only one of primary elections. Fortunately, a few political scientists have sought to raise the

[44] Some leading statements of these early anti-direct primary views are: Emanuel L. Philipp (La Follette's chief "Stalwart" adversary in Wisconsin), *Political Reform in Wisconsin* (Milwaukee, Wisc: published by the author, 1910); Karl J. Geiser, "Defects in the Direct Primary," *Annals of the American Academy of Political and Social Science*, 106 (March, 1923), 31-39; Arnold Bennett Hall, "The Direct Primary and Party Responsibility," *Annals*, 40-54; and Daniel S. Remsen, *Primary Elections* (New York: G.P. Putnam's Sons, 1894).

[45] Key's work is published mainly in *Southern Politics in State and Nation* (New York: Alfred A. Knopf, 1949), and *American State Politics: An Introduction* (New York: Alfred A. Knopf, 1956). The other leading citations are: Cortez A.M. Ewing, *Primary Elections in the South* (Norman, Okla.: University of Oklahoma Press, 1953); Andrew Hacker, "Does a 'Divisive' Primary Harm a Candidate's Election Chances?", *American Political Science Review*, 59 (March, 1965), 105-110; Frank J. Sorauf, *Party and Representation* (New York: Atherton Press, 1963); William H. Standing and James A. Robinson, "Inter-Party Competition and Primary Contesting: The Case of Indiana," *American Political Science Review*, 52 (December, 1958), 1066-1078; and Julius Turner, "Primary Elections as the Alternatives to Party Competition in 'Safe' Districts," *Journal of Politics*, 15 (1953), 197-210.

discussion of primaries above the assertion-and-counterassertion level of their original advocates and opponents. The most notable work has been done by V.O. Key, but useful contributions have also come from Cortez Ewing, Andrew Hacker, Frank Sorauf, William Standing and James Robinson, and Julius Turner.[45] Leon Epstein and I have also used survey data to investigate how persons who vote in primaries resemble and differ from those who do not.[46]

In my judgment these studies warrant at least some observations about how direct primaries really operate. First, by no means all primaries are contested, and whether the voters have a choice depends upon two main factors: competition is less likely if an incumbent is running for renomination, and less likely if it is thought the nominee has no chance of winning the general election. Hence it is not unusual for there to be no candidates or only one candidate in, say, Republican primaries in Mississippi and Democratic primaries in Vermont.[47]

Second, voting turnout is much lower in primaries than in general elections. For example, the mean turnout in gubernatorial and senatorial primaries in the two-party states between 1962 and 1968 was 28 percent, compared with 61 percent in their ensuing general elections;[48] and in the eleven state presidential primaries contested in both parties in the period from 1948 to 1968, the mean turnout

[46] Austin Ranney and Leon D. Epstein, "The Two Electorates: Voters and Non-Voters in a Wisconsin Primary," *Journal of Politics*, 28 (August, 1966), 598-616; Ranney, "The Representativeness of Primary Electorates," *Midwest Journal of Political Science*, 12 (May, 1968), 224-238; and Ranney, "Turnout and Representation in Presidential Primary Elections," *American Political Science Review*, 66 (March, 1972), 21-37.

[47] Cf. Key, *American State Politics*, pp. 104-118; Standing and Robinson, *op. cit.*; and Turner, *op. cit.*

[48] Austin Ranney, "Parties in State Politics," Herbert Jacob and Kenneth Vines (ed.), *Politics in the American States* (2d ed., Boston: Little, Brown, 1971), Table 3, p. 98.

was 39 percent, compared to 69 percent in the same states' general elections.[49] I think the reason is clear. In the United States as in other Western democracies, the principal factor "structuring the vote" is the candidates' party labels. That is, for most ordinary voters the single strongest cue for making sense out of the "booming, buzzing confusion" of names and issues confronting them is their preference for one party or another. Hence a candidate's party label is for most of us a clear sign that he is either a good guy or a bad guy, a sign not likely to be overridden except in those few cases in which the candidate's individual qualities are widely known even to people not very interested in politics. But in primary elections there are no labels by the candidates' names. For a voter registered in that party they are all good guys, and it really makes little difference which of them takes on the bad guy in the general election. So why bother to vote in the primary? The turnout evidence shows that most people don't.[50]

Third, the few people who do vote in primaries are in several respects quite unrepresentative of the many who do not. They are richer and better educated; they are more interested in politics; and they are more likely to have strong opinions on the issues and personalities of the day. It is not clear whether they tend to favor candidates and issue positions different from those of their nonvoting fellow partisans. Key believed that they do:

> the effective primary constituency may often be a caricature of the entire party following. . . . [It] may

[49] Ranney, "Turnout and Representation in Presidential Primary Elections," Table 1, p. 24.

[50] For evidence on the vote-structuring role of party labels, see Leon D. Epstein, *Political Parties in Western Democracies* (New York: Frederick A. Praeger, 1967), Ch. IV; Angus Campbell, Philip E. Converse, Warren E. Miller, and Donald E. Stokes, *The American Voter* (New York: John Wiley & Sons, 1960), pp. 142-143; and Don R. Bowen, *Political Behavior of the American Public* (Columbus, Ohio: Charles E. Merrill, 1968), p. 129.

come to consist predominantly of the people of certain sections of a state, of persons chiefly of specified national origin or religious affiliation, of people especially responsive to certain styles of political leadership or shades of ideology, or of other groups markedly unrepresentative in one way or another of the party following.... Under some circumstances the miniscule and unrepresentative primary constituency may project its features upon the party leadership and handicap the party in polling the maximum party strength in the general election.[51]

Leon Epstein and I found little evidence of this among voters and nonvoters in the Wisconsin gubernatorial primaries of 1964 and 1966, but this may have reflected the low ideological content of those particular contests. Our later study of the more intense Wisconsin and New Hampshire presidential primaries in 1968 did reveal some of the traits that Key feared. So there is some smoke to be seen in the vicinity Key predicted; how hot and dangerous is the fire producing it we cannot say—at least not on the basis of any first-hand inspection of the flames made yet.

However, few political scientists refrain from saying something about important questions they cannot answer perfectly, so let me add my own impressions to those of Key and other students of primaries. For one, it seems to me that the direct primary in most instances has not only eliminated boss control of nominations but party control as well. Whatever may have been the case before the La Follette revolution, there are today no officers or committees in the national parties and very few in the state and local parties who can regularly give nominations to some aspirants and withhold them from others. To be sure, in many states party committees and leaders often publicly endorse particular primary candidates, and my

[51] *American State Politics*, pp. 152-153.

impression is that those endorsed win more often than they lose. Yet it is equally common for party organizations to make no endorsements or other visible efforts to support particular aspirants; and even when they do it is not unusual for a well-known and well-financed "outsider" to beat them. A few of the better known recent examples are Pierre Salinger in California, Milton Shapp in Pennsylvania, and Dan Walker in Illinois.

How did our parties become so weak? How much credit—or blame—should we assign to direct primaries? Perhaps La Follette and the Progressive reformers had their facts wrong, and American parties have always been unbossed. Or perhaps they would have become what they are even if there had never been a direct primary. But I find it hard to dispute Key's judgment:

> The adoption of the direct primary opened the road for disruptive forces that gradually fractionalized the party organization. By permitting more effective direct appeals by individual politicians to the party membership, the primary system freed forces driving toward the disintegration of party organizations and facilitated the construction of factions and cliques attached to the ambitions of individual leaders. The convention system compelled leaders to treat, to deal, to allocate nominations; the primary permits individual aspirants by one means or another to build a wider following within the party. . . .
>
> Indeed, the fact that aspirants for nomination must cultivate the rank and file makes it difficult to maintain an organizational core dedicated to the party as such; instead, leadership energies operate to construct activist clusters devoted to the interests of particular individuals[52]

[52] V.O. Key, Jr., *Politics, Parties & Pressure Groups* (5th ed., New York: Thomas Y. Crowell, 1964), pp. 342, 386.

Curing the Mischiefs of Faction

Leon Epstein disagrees. He suggests that the direct primary is more a symptom than a cause—that it has not made the parties what they are but rather is itself a result of the fact that "Americans have not wanted to leave the selection of their party candidates entirely in the hands of organized partisans." That, he says, is why they fought corruption in party organizations, not by substituting a new kind of organization, but by bypassing party organization altogether.[53]

Even so, the question remains: *why* did they choose that particular path? A good part of the answer, I believe, is found in the American ambivalence toward parties discussed in Chapter 2. It seems we want party labels on our ballots to help us distinguish the good guys from the bad guys, but we do not want the decisions about who gets the labels made by small gangs of politicians: we all know what kind of people *they* are. That being the case, perhaps the direct primary is the best way to keep the parties weak without destroying them altogether. If that is our basic view, it would make primaries characteristically American institutions in more ways than one.

4. *A National Presidential Primary?* Whatever may be our reasons for adopting and preserving the direct primary, and however we may assay its effects, it is surely here to stay. It is decades since any state abandoned the primary or reduced its coverage, and what little change there has been in recent years has been the move in a few states (e.g., Connecticut and New York) to increase the coverage of primaries. And, as we observed earlier, eight states have instituted presidential primaries since 1969.

The most recent demonstration of the direct primary's appeal is the current revival of proposals for a national presidential primary. The idea of legally imposing direct democracy upon the national parties was, as we might

[53] Epstein, *op. cit.*, pp. 210-211.

expect, born in the Progressive era, and was first formally proposed by Woodrow Wilson in his initial message to Congress in 1913.[54] Little was heard of it for three decades thereafter, but the agonies of presidential politics in 1948 and 1952 touched off another round of proposals, including separate bills introduced in the Senate between 1953 and 1961 by George Smathers, Paul Douglas, Estes Kefauver, William Proxmire, and Margaret Chase Smith.

After that, all was quiet until 1972 when another round of bills was introduced. Their details need not detain us long, but we should note that three main variants have been proposed. Senators Mike Mansfield and George Aiken and Representatives Gerald Ford and Silvio Conte have introduced bills establishing a national presidential primary to be held throughout the entire nation on one day, with a runoff election to follow if no candidate receives more than 40 percent of the popular vote on the first go-round. A second variant has been proposed by Senator Robert Packwood: his bill would hold primaries in the states of each of five regions in successive months; after each round of primaries each candidate would appoint a number of national convention delegates from each state proportional to his share of the popular vote in the state; and the convention would choose the nominee. The third variant, in a bill introduced by Representative Morris Udall, would not compel the states to hold presidential primaries, but would require those which did to choose one of only three permissible dates in the period from April through June. A candidate receiving a majority of a state's votes would get all of its delegates; otherwise they would be distributed proportionally among the leading candidates.[55]

[54] The most comprehensive survey of the early proposals is Louise Overacker, *The Presidential Primary* (New York: Macmillan, 1926).
[55] The various bills are summarized in *Congressional Quarterly Weekly Report*, July 8, 1972, pp. 1650-1654. For a popular presentation

Making the Parties Behave

It seems clear why these proposals came when they did. Back in 1968 when only fifteen states and the District of Columbia held presidential primaries and when less than half of the conventions' delegates were so chosen or bound, most congressmen, like most political scientists, thought that the "mix" was preferable to either a national primary or no primaries at all.[56] But many were appalled by the increase in expense and drain on the candidates' energies and reputations in 1972 created by the addition of the seven new primaries. Many politicians and academics still agree with the McGovern-Fraser commission's conclusion that truly representative conventions are preferable to a national primary.[57] But some have come to feel that few, if any, of the states are going to repeal their primaries; and, if that is so, then almost anything—even a national primary—would be better than the present mess. Moreover, a national primary seems to be what the people want: a Gallup poll taken in mid-May, 1972, found 72 percent favoring a national primary, 10 percent undecided, and only 18 percent opposed.[58]

Thus it is clear that from the 1790s to today many Americans have rejected efforts to make the parties more representative because they believed the only worthy goal to be that of achieving true intraparty direct democracy. However, there has been a third group which all along

---

of the case for the national presidential primary see Leonard Lurie, *The King Makers* (New York: Coward, McCann, and Geoghegan, 1971), pp. 259-262.

[56] Cf. Nelson W. Polsby and Aaron B. Wildavsky, *Presidential Elections: Strategies of American Electoral Politics* (2d ed., New York: Charles Scribner's Sons, 1968), pp. 238-239; James W. Davis, *Presidential Primaries: Road to the White House* (New York: Thomas Y. Crowell, 1967), pp. 269-271; and Gerald Pomper, *Nominating the President* (New York: W.W. Norton, 1966), pp. 230, 275-276.

[57] See *Mandate for Reform*, pp. 11-12.

[58] Reported in *Congressional Quarterly Weekly Report*, July 8, 1972, p. 1651.

has insisted that the ultimate criterion for judging a party's organization is not whether it is truly representative or ideally democratic, but whether it puts the party in the best possible condition to win elections. I shall conclude by examining this view

ORGANIZING PARTIES TO WIN ELECTIONS

EXPRESSIVENESS V. COMPETITIVENESS

The representativeness and direct-democracy ideals have in common the fact that they give top priority to what might be called the *expressive* function of party organization. That is, their main standard for judging a party's institutions is how accurately they express certain characteristics of the party members: their biological and social traits or their candidate and issue preferences—or, as in the McGovern-Fraser commission's stance, both. There is no end of disagreement among them about just who *are* the party members whose characteristics should be expressed, and their differing views on this question will be our main concern in the next chapter. But they do agree on the fundamental proposition that a party's first duty is, in some fashion, to express the nature and will of its members.

Both views have been challenged by those who give top priority to what might be called the *competitive* function of party organization. Their main criterion for judging party institutions is how effectively they mobilize the party's resources for winning elections. They do not ask whether representativeness is *in itself* a higher or lower value than direct democracy. They ask rather which—if either—best enables the party to choose the candidates most attractive, not to its own activists, but to the voters whose support it needs to win. They also seek the best arrangements for recruiting the workers and collecting the money to make the best campaign. The end is winning elections, the primary means is "combat effectiveness," and reform and antireform alike are judged according to whether they contribute to or detract from that effectiveness. This view, let us be clear, was not invented recently by those who oppose the McGovern-Fraser commission's reforms, nor seventy years ago by those who fought the Progressives. It has played a major role in all disputes over party reform from the beginning.

As we have seen, the Republican party was founded by Madison and Jefferson in the 1790s to get more opponents of Hamilton's policies elected to Congress and other public offices. Its basic technique was to designate candidates for elective offices so as to concentrate and thus make effective anti-Hamilton sentiment among the voters. Its Federalist opponents were forced to follow suit, and both parties were widely condemned both from the left (by John Taylor of Caroline) and from the right (by George Washington) for dividing the nation and interfering with the people's right to rule.

The legislative and congressional caucuses soon took over the major nominations, and they too were widely attacked as unrepresentative and undemocratic. Some politicians who participated in these party operations were evidently chary of publicly defending what they were doing, but some courageous souls proclaimed that party organization was indispensable to the preservation and advancement of the great principles they believed in. Thus the sixty-six Congressmen who braved public scorn to participate in the last congressional caucus nomination in 1824 issued this statement:

> It is now twenty-four years since the great political revolution [which brought the Republican party to power] was effected, and the power which was then

135

acquired by republicans in the government of the union is still retained. Their enjoyment of this ascendancy has not, however, been undisturbed; on the contrary, they have had an unwearied struggle to maintain with the same adversary over whom their triumph was achieved. It is not to be doubted that it was by union and concert of action that the strength of the republican unity was consolidated, and its success in the decisive controversy effected. It is as little to be doubted, that it is by adherence to the same principle and policy of action that its unbroken force and continued ascendancy can be preserved.[59]

Now this argument had made good sense in the days when the Federalists were thought to be a real threat to the Republicans, but it seemed to most an anachronism in 1824 when there was no Federalist candidate or even party. Historical "if's" may be futile exercises, but one cannot help speculating that if two-party competition had survived into the 1820s the congressional caucus might well have survived too. In that case the sharp break between the "presidential party" and "congressional party" created by Jackson's triumph in 1828 and enhanced by the establishment of the national conventions in 1831-1832 might never have occurred—with who knows what consequences for the subsequent development of the parties and indeed of the whole political system.[60]

In any case, the new state and national conventions were at first generally praised as being more representative than the legislative caucuses. But they soon came under attack for being boss-ridden, unrepresentative, and the main source of evil in American politics—an attack which,

[59] Quoted in *Niles' Weekly Register*, Vol. 25, February 21, 1824, p. 390. See also Charles S. Sydnor, "The One-Party Period of American History," *American Historical Review*, 51 (April. 1946), 443-445.

[60] Cf. the speculation by David, Goldman, and Bain, *op. cit.*, p. 17.

as we have seen, led to the general adoption of the direct primary in the twentieth century. But from the 1830s to now, some commentators, most recently Herbert McClosky, have praised the conventions, not because they are ideally expressive but because they are effective institutions for nominating able candidates who have wide voter appeal and for unifying the parties behind them.[61]

Some historians contend that the early conventions performed these functions even better than the legislative caucuses had.[62] One of the most powerful arguments in the Progressive era for conventions over direct primaries was that conventions, like legislatures, encourage negotiation and accommodation among the parties' contending factions, while primaries, like referenda, are uncompromisable struggles to the death among adversaries who cannot yield. An early version of McClosky's case was well put by Arnold Bennett Hall, an anti-La Follette member of the University of Wisconsin faculty:

> [One] reason why compromise is essential in the nomination of candidates is that unless there is such a spirit of accommodation and adjustment, the party will be driven upon the rocks of factional disaster, and party responsibility disappears. In a nominating convention, the majority, while insisting upon a candidate that supports their views, are generally careful to avoid candidates that are so extreme as to tempt the minority to bolt the ticket. In this way extreme candidates are generally avoided, and the coherent unity of the party is maintained. Under the primary system, where there is no chance for conference, adjustment and compromise, but where it is an indi-

[61] Herbert McClosky, "Are Political Conventions Undemocratic?", *New York Times Magazine*, August 4, 1968, pp. 15-21.

[62] Cf. Chase, *op. cit.*, pp. 234-235; Luetscher, *op. cit.*, pp. 79-81; and McCormick, *op. cit.*, pp. 346-349.

vidual scramble for votes, candidates representing the opposite extremes have frequently been nominated on the ticket.[63]

Some may feel that these praises for the convention system sound strange in the light of what the 1972 Democratic national convention did and what may have been its consequences for the party's horrendous defeat in the election. But let us remember that the McGovern-Fraser commission's rules, which did so much to shape the composition and product of that convention, were not mainly, if at all, intended to maximize the party's competitiveness. The commission's report made it perfectly clear that they had other priorities:

> The Guidelines that we have adopted are designed to eliminate the inequities in the delegate selection process. . . . We view popular participation as the lifeblood of the National Convention system; any compromise with this threatens the future of the Convention. . . . We believe that popular participation is more than a proud heritage of our party, more even than a first principle. We believe that popular control of the Democratic Party is necessary for its survival. . . . If we are not an open party; if we do not represent the demands of change, then the danger is not that people will go to the Republican Party; it is that there will no longer be a way for people committed to orderly change to fulfill their needs and desires within our traditional political system. It is that they will turn to third and fourth party politics or the anti-politics of the street.[64]

By its own account, then, the McGovern-Fraser commission was not seeking ways of merely winning elections;

[63] Arnold Bennett Hall, *op. cit.*, pp. 52-53.
[64] *Mandate for Reform*, pp. 33, 49.

it sought to save the whole political and party system by making the Democratic party more expressive. Whatever one may think of these value priorities and this understanding of the political system's dangers in 1972, the historical fact is that not only in 1969-1972 but in most other conflicts over party reform in America from the 1820s to now, the values of expressiveness have usually overshadowed the values of competitiveness. Whether they will continue to do so remains to be seen.

"PURISTS" V. "PROFESSIONALS" IN THE 1960s AND 1970s

Nelson Polsby and Aaron Wildavsky make a convincing case for the proposition that since the early 1960s, conflict within both national parties has increasingly become a contest between people they classify as "purists" and "professionals."[65] The "purists" are people who previously have had little to do with party politics and become active to support a particular presidential aspirant because he is identified with their own deeply held positions on issues. Such people won the Republican nomination for Barry Goldwater in 1964 and the Democratic nomination for George McGovern in 1972; and they were the main supporters of Eugene McCarthy in 1968 and George Wallace in 1972. Polsby and Wildavsky interviewed samples of Goldwater and McCarthy delegates and found that their differences in ideology were far less significant than their agreement about what constitutes proper political behavior. The party itself, they believe, has no value and merits no loyalty. Its only legitimate reason for being is to advance true ideals and good policies. The essence of politics is not the mere competition for office among parties and interest groups; it is standing up and being counted for what is right regardless of whether it is popular. Any

[65] Polsby and Wildavsky, *op. cit.* (3d ed., New York: Charles Scribner's Sons, 1971), pp. 35-59.

compromise or soft-pedalling of principle is immoral, hypocritical, and a sure sign of a candidate's unfitness for the nomination. Hence the candidacy of a Goldwater or a McCarthy or a McGovern or a Wallace is not to be judged by whether he won or lost, but by whether he stuck to his principles.

Opposed to them have been the "professionals." Their differences from the purists were eloquently set forth by the playwright Arthur Miller, himself a purist and a McCarthy delegate from Connecticut in 1968. He explained the violence surrounding that convention thus:

> There had to be violence for many reasons, but one fundamental cause was the two opposite ideas of politics in this Democratic party. The professionals—the ordinary Senator, congressman, State Committeeman, Mayor, officeholder—see politics as a sort of game in which you win sometimes and sometimes you lose. Issues are not something you feel, like morality, like good and evil, but something you succeed or fail to make use of. To these men an issue is a segment of public opinion which you either capitalize on or attempt to assuage according to the present interests of the party. To the amateurs—the McCarthy people and some of the Kennedy adherents —an issue is first of all moral, and embodies a vision of the country, even of man, and is not a counter in a game. The great majority of the men and women at the convention were delegates from the party to the party.[66]

Polsby and Wildavsky do not quote Miller, but his revulsion accords with their analysis. The professionals

[66] Arthur Miller, "The Battle of Chicago: From the Delegates' Side," *New York Times Magazine*, September 15, 1968, p. 29.

are people who have a substantial commitment to the party itself. They have served it before the nomination contest and expect to serve it after the election. They regard threats to bolt the party as dirty pool; their morality requires the candidates and factions to compete in good faith and the losers to unite behind the winners—though a particularly unsuitable candidate may incline even the professionals to "go fishing" on election day. Winning the election is the party's prime goal, for it is an indispensable prerequisite for everything else it wants to do. Therefore the professionals seek a candidate whose style they think will appeal to the voters they need to win, not necessarily to party leaders. They judge a candidate by how well or badly he runs in the election and by how much he has helped or hurt the rest of the ticket. And they see negotiation, compromise, and accommodation not as hypocrisy or immorality but as the very essence of what keeps parties—and nations—from disintegrating.

Like Polsby and Wildavsky, I realize that these are Weberian "ideal types" and that few real-life politicians are entirely unsullied purists or unprincipled professionals. As we saw in Chapter 2, most McGovernites were willing to set aside some of their most cherished proposals for the platform in order to improve their man's chances of winning; and their leader was willing—indeed, eager—to mend his fences with that arch-professional, Mayor Richard J. Daley. By the same token, John Connally and his Democrats for Nixon were mainly professionals who found their party's candidate and platform so unacceptable that they bolted to the opposition, some of them permanently. Both the McGovernites and the Connallyites had plenty of precedents for their deviations from perfect purism and complete professionalism.

Even so, I believe that Polsby and Wildavsky—and Arthur Miller too—are quite correct in describing Republican presidential politics in 1964 and Democratic presidential politics in 1968 as mainly clashes between the two attitudes. It seems to me that was also the case with the Democrats in 1972. Even more, my reading of American political history suggests that much of its conflict over party reform in all periods can be understood as a three-cornered dispute among purists-for-representativeness, purists-for-direct-democracy, and professionals-for-competitiveness. The next round has already begun with the introduction of legislation for a national presidential primary, and its pace will surely quicken in 1974 and beyond.

I do not know what the outcome will be. But I do expect that it will be decided, as all the past trilateral conflicts over party reform have been, by how much support each of the three sides can muster and by what alliances each can manage with one or another of its competitors. From this perspective all conflict over party reform is, in the end, a struggle for putting the right people in charge. That will be our focus in the next chapter.

CHAPTER FIVE

Putting the Right People in Charge

On January 15, 1953, Mr. Charles E. Wilson added a memorable phrase to the folklore of American politics. The Senate Armed Services Committee was examining his fitness to be Secretary of Defense, and a Senator asked him what he would do if a conflict arose between the interests of his former employer and the national interest. Wilson made headlines by replying, "I cannot conceive of [such a conflict], because for years I have thought that what was good for our country was good for General Motors, *and vice versa.*[1]

I well remember how we liberal Democrats deplored his ethics and jeered at his naiveté in blurting this out in public. After all, American liberals, progressives, and reformers in general have ever been alert to the false pretences, weasel words, and blatant lies of our conservative opponents. We have not been fooled by their protestations of concern for the public interest, because we know they are smokescreens to mask selfishness. But we have never had a monopoly of such worldly wisdom; we have shared

[1] New York *Times*, January 24, 1953, p. 8, emphasis added.

143

it with radicals, conservatives, reactionaries—indeed, with all Americans. However different may be the lines of political goods we peddle, the one thing we all believe is that whatever the other sides *say*, they are all in fact looking out for themselves, every day of the week and twice on Sundays.

And so they are. We observed in Chapter 3 that throughout the history of conflict over party reform in America it has been impossible to separate the feelings about changes in the rules from their policy and candidate preferences. Could it be otherwise? Do not all of us support the candidates and policies we do because we believe they will be good for our party and the nation? Political victory may not be our only or our ultimate goal, but it surely is a highly useful means for achieving whatever goals we have. Accordingly, most of us support the rules we think will help our side and oppose those we think will hurt us. This is not hypocrisy or callousness. It is prudence. The influence of rules on outcomes is a fact of political life, and we must accept it if our policy and candidate preferences are to be anything more than chatter. Let us confess, then, that if we are serious about politics we all have our own versions of Secretary Wilson's famous dictum.

From this perspective all conflict over party reform is, at bottom, conflict over who should be running the parties, and through them the nation. The issue has been most manifest in the perennial disputes over who should be treated as party *members*. The membership issue underlies most of the quarrels over how the parties should be organized and their decisions made. For example, if the prime goal is descriptive representation of the members' characteristics, then we must choose which ones to represent. Age? Race? Sex? Income? Party service? Or, if the object is to represent the members' candidate preferences and issue positions, *whose* views should be reflected? The people whose votes the party needs to win? The activists who work for candidates and causes? The party regulars? Or, if the goal is direct rule by the parties' members in primaries, who should be allowed to vote? Any qualified voter, as in Wisconsin? Any voter who publicly requests the party's primary ballot, as in Illinois? Only those voters previously registered as party members, as in California? Or only dues-paying, card-carrying party members, as in Norway and Belgium?

In short, just about every conflict over making the parties more representative or more democratic or more responsive or more effective turns on the basic question of who should be treated as party members. We shall begin this chapter by identifying the principal answers to this question given in America and elsewhere.

IDENTIFYING THE PARTIES' MEMBERS

One way to tackle the question of the "true" nature of party membership is to identify the characteristics of "membership" of other social organizations and apply them to the parties. But this turns out to be a good deal harder than it sounds. Webster's definition of "member" focuses on a person's formal admission to the organization and his consequent assumption of obligations to it and receipt of privileges from it:

> [A "member" is] one of the individuals composing a society, community, association, or another group: as. . . . (1) a person who has been admitted usually formally to the responsibilities and privileges of some association or joint enterprise. . . .(2) a person who has been admitted usually formally into some social or professional society typically requiring payment of

dues, adherence to a program, or compliance with some other requirements of membership.[2]

This dictionary definition can be illustrated by the qualifications for membership of a church or a corporation or a labor union, but a political scientist may be pardoned for thinking first of the concept of citizenship, which is membership of a nation-state. At first glance the legal concept of a citizen is quite simple: it is a person who gives allegiance to a nation and receives protection and the privilege of participation in its political affairs. But a closer look reveals that each nation imposes its own standards, and as a result many people are citizens of more than one nation while others are "stateless," that is, citizens of none.[3] Moreover, we know there are some kinds of membership which are largely informal but memberships all the same—as, for example, membership of a circle of friends, or an audience.

Social scientists who study membership in organized and unorganized human groups generally stress some kind of commonality or ties among the persons concerned. They distinguish among "communicative," "normative," and "functional" ties; but these ties can be so loose and tenuous that the boundaries between the members and non-members of particular groups often become hopelessly blurred.[4] Unfortunately, then, the legal and social science

[2] *Webster's Third International Dictionary* (Springfield, Mass.: G. & C. Merriam, 1966), p. 1408.
[3] Cf. United Nations Legislative Service, *Laws Concerning Nationality* (New York: United Nations Publications, 1954), and H. Mark Roelofs, *The Tensions of Citizenship* (New York: Holt, Rinehart and Winston, 1957).
[4] Some leading items in the vast literature on the subject are: George C. Homans, *The Human Group* (New York: Harcourt, Brace, 1950); Dorwin Cartwright and Alvin Zander (ed.), *Group Dynamics: Research and Theory* (2d ed., Evanston, Ill.: Row, Peterson, 1960); James G. March and Herbert A. Simon, *Organizations* (New York: John Wiley & Sons, 1958); and Peter M. Blau and W. Richard Scott, *Formal*

literature on the general concept of "membership" does not furnish clear and unambiguous standards which we can use to settle the question of who should be treated as party members. So we ask next: what standards do American and European party politicians apply?

PARTY MEMBERSHIP IN WESTERN DEMOCRACIES

Most political scientists' discussions of party membership[5] begin with Maurice Duverger's well-known distinction between "cadre" and "mass" parties. A cadre party, he says, consists of a few self-selected activists who make the party's decisions. It has no formal membership list or procedures for admission and collects no dues. One "joins" such a party simply by participating in its activities. This, he observes, is the way most of the world's center and right-of-center parties are organized.

A mass party, on the other hand, has a formal procedure for admitting—and expelling—party members and maintains an official roster of those currently in good standing. The members formally promise to support the party's principles and candidates, pay regular dues, and carry cards attesting to their membership. Most of the world's socialist parties are so organized, although a few moderate and conservative parties have followed their example in what Duverger calls "contagion from the Left."[6]

Organizations: A Comparative Approach (San Francisco: Chandler, 1962).

[5] The most comprehensive surveys are: Maurice Duverger, *Political Parties: Their Organization and Activity in the Modern State*, translated from the French by Barbara and Robert North (New York: John Wiley & Sons, 1954), Book I, Ch. 2; and Leon D. Epstein, *Political Parties in Western Democracies* (New York: Frederick A. Praeger, 1967), esp. pp. 111-122, 250-256. See also Frank J. Sorauf, *Political Parties in the American System* (Boston: Little, Brown, 1964), pp. 44-48.

[6] Duverger, *op. cit.*, pp. 62-65, 71-74.

Whatever may be the utility of these categories for classifying the parties of Western Europe, American parties fit them awkwardly if at all. Duverger concludes, for instance, that the parties in the states with "closed" direct primaries resemble mass parties in some ways and cadre parties in others.[7] And other scholars have pointed out that some states, notably California, New York, and Wisconsin, have both "statutory parties," which are organized according to the law with one kind of membership rules, and "extralegal parties," which are organized outside the law with quite different membership rules.[8]

But we need not wander in this analytical maze any longer. Identifying what *is* the nature of party membership in the United States and comparing it with its counterparts in other Western nations is a matter of interest mainly to scholars. But deciding what *should be* the qualifications for party membership is today, as it always has been, a basic issue—perhaps *the* basic issue—for all who participate in disputes over party reform.

FACING UP TO THE ISSUE

Despite its critical importance for most quarrels over party reform, the membership issue has rarely been faced directly and explicitly by the adherents of any side. For example, Robert M. LaFollette's first speeches advocating the direct primary in 1897 and 1898 clearly proposed that each party's primary should be closed to all but the party's members. The states should, he said,

provide that when each voter enters the election booth on primary election day he shall find a committee of his party in charge of a separate ballot box and the official primary election ballot upon which is

[7] *Ibid.*, p. 65.
[8] Epstein, *op. cit.*, pp. 122-126; Sorauf, *op. cit.*, pp. 45-47.

printed the names of all candidates of his party for nomination. [States should also] provide that each voter may take the ballot of the party with which he affiliates, and in private, indicate thereon the names of the men who are his choice as the nominees of his party, and he may then deposit that ballot in the ballot box of his party.[9]

But, a mere three years later, his first gubernatorial message to the Wisconsin legislature proposed legislation establishing an *open* primary—that is, one in which there is no party registration, the voter is given the ballots of both parties, marks whichever he chooses, and deposits it without any public disclosure of which party he has chosen.[10] I have found no statements by La Follette or anyone else explaining this major switch from his original proposals, but it is enshrined, perhaps forever, in Wisconsin's laws and political culture.

However, no former member of the McGovern-Fraser commission, like myself, is entitled to criticize La Follette for not have squarely and explicitly faced the membership question. Our commission wanted to make the party's national conventions "more representative," and our decisions on a good many reform proposals rested upon a certain conception of who is a Democrat and hence entitled to be represented in the party's presidential candidate selection process. Yet, without ever directly discussing that conception or its alternatives, we required "representation of minority groups, young people, and women in reasonable relationship to their presence in the population of the State." We required the state parties to appor-

[9] Speech at the University of Michigan, March 12, 1898, quoted in Allen F. Lovejoy, *La Follette and the Establishment of the Direct Primary in Wisconsin, 1890-1904* (New Haven, Conn.: Yale University Press, 1941), p. 45.

[10] *Laws of Wisconsin* (1903), Ch. 451, p. 766.

tion their conventions "on a formula giving equal weight to total population and to the Democratic vote in the previous presidential election." We prohibited all ex officio delegate slots for public or party officeholders. And the nearest we ever came to stating our definition of who is a Democrat was this rather permissive statement in Guideline C-3:

> The Commission believes that Party membership, and hence opportunity to participate in the delegate selection process, must be open to all persons who wish to be Democrats and who are not already members of another political party. . . .[11]

So the McGovern-Fraser commission, like nearly every other participant in conflicts over party reform throughout American history, had little to say about its underlying conception of party membership. Yet the arguments made for and against various reform proposals from the earliest days to now clearly stem from one or another of four quite different and competing conceptions. I shall review them in the order of their inclusiveness.

AMERICAN CONCEPTIONS OF PARTY MEMBERSHIP

1. *Party Regulars.* In Chapter 4 I borrowed heavily from Polsby and Wildavsky's descriptions of the "purists" and "professionals" in the national conventions of 1964 and 1968.[12] One of the main differences between the two types is how they feel about the issue of whether prior party service should confer a special right to participate in making the party's decisions.

[11] Guideline C-3, Commission on Party Structure and Delegate Selection, *Mandate for Reform* (Washington, D.C.: Democratic National Committee, 1970), p. 47. The other quotations are from, respectively, Guidelines A-1 and A-2, p. 40; B-7, p. 45; and C-2, p. 46.

[12] Nelson W. Polsby and Aaron B. Wildavsky, *Presidential Elections: Strategies of American Electoral Politics* (3d ed., New York: Charles Scribner's Sons, 1971), pp. 35-59.

Putting the Right People in Charge

The "professionals" believe that a party's conventions should be composed of and its nominations made by people who have *earned* the right by regular service to the party in the past and by a firm intention to continue serving it in the future. They feel one's commitment to the party should be lifelong, and any particular dispute over a platform or a nomination should be seen as one episode among many. Perhaps your faction will lose this time, they say, but you will always have a chance to win next time. And win or lose at any time, you should stick with the party. Any threat to walk out if your candidate or pet issue loses is a kind of political blackmail that in itself shows you do not deserve a voice in party affairs.

This view has been expressed from the very beginnings of our party system. For example, in 1803 the Republican Committee of Bucks County, Pennsylvania, published an "address" exhorting its partisans to support the party's ticket regardless of whether they approved every last name on it:

> Would you merit the character of Republicans? Bow to the will of the majority, and support the ticket formed by your representatives. . . .Cleave to the system of Republican union, as to the horns of freedom's altar. . . .Take the obvious means to extend your power and influence, and do not madly pull down with your own hands the fabric you created with so much care. In fine, would you disappoint the hopes of your enemies, and avoid the ridicule which awaits your fall? Make your Committee a just representation of the Republican interest—support by your votes the ticket they recommend—and take for your pole star that political maxim, United We Stand, Divided We Fall.[13]

[13] Quoted in George D. Luetscher, "Early Political Machinery in

The same view was put in somewhat less reverberating prose by William L. Marcy, one of Van Buren's "new breed" of pragmatic party regulars in the late 1820s:

An opposition to a candidate which is abstractly right may be politically wrong. . . .The example of opposing a candidate nominated by political friends is bad not only as to its effect on the pending election but as to others that are to succeed it. An opposition upon the ground of principle will be used to authorize an opposition on the ground of caprice.[14]

Polsby and Wildavsky have found these sentiments most clearly articulated in our own time by some Humphrey delegates at the 1968 Democratic Convention:

The McWhinnies [McCarthy supporters] are like little boys with marbles; you don't play by their rules—they want to break up the game. . . .The party structure is always open to people who are interested in working. . . .It's just that we have a sort of seniority system like Congress; those who make the most contribution get the largest say in what we do. That's only fair. . . .The problem is that while the McCarthy kids want into the party they want in at the top. They aren't interested in the status which the beginner usually gets licking envelopes and things like that, which we did, all of us, when we were coming up.[15]

2. *Candidate and Issue Enthusiasts.* Polsby and Wildavsky's interviews with the Goldwater and McCarthy

---

the United States" (Philadelphia: University of Pennsylvania Ph.D. thesis, 1903), pp. 80-81.

[14] Quoted in Richard Hofstadter, *The Idea of a Party System* (Berkeley, Los Angeles and London: University of Californi Press, 1970), p. 245.

[15] Quoted in Polsby and Wildavsky, *op. cit.*, p. 44.

delegates in 1964 and 1968 found a very different conception of party membership among the "purists." They believed that the convention should be composed of people who are committed to particular candidates and issue stands in the year of the convention. Blind loyalty to the party itself is not only foolish but immoral. If the party nominates a good candidate on a good platform, it deserves support; but if it nominates a bad candidate on a bad platform, it should be opposed and it deserves to lose. In short, ask not whether this year's candidate enthusiasts and issue enthusiasts deserve to be delegates; ask rather whether the party's ticket and platform deserve their support.

Thus the Goldwater delegates said of their man, "He is straightforward; he doesn't compromise; he doesn't pander to the public; he's against expedience." And the McCarthy delegates said of theirs, "he's sincere and honest. He opposed the war in the primaries, and he's not a bullshitter. He wouldn't sell out. He won't compromise."[16]

These attitudes are closely related to the conception of party membership implicit in the McGovern-Fraser commission's report and guidelines. The commission rejected the notion that past party service should give any special advantage to a person seeking to be a national convention delegate. Most of the guidelines were consciously designed to maximize participation by persons who are enthusiasts for a particular presidential aspirant or policy *in the year of the convention*. Whatever the would-be delegate has done for the party in the past was rendered irrelevant to his chances for selection in the convention year. The commission sought these goals by banning all devices which in the past had epecially favored party regulars or "insiders": e.g., the reservation of ex

[16] *Ibid.*, pp. 37, 41.

officio delegate slots for the party's governors, senators, congressmen, state chairmen, and national committeemen and committeewomen.[17] The commission also tried to eliminate any secrecy and complexity in the selection procedures that might give old hands an advantage over new enthusiasts.[18]

The guidelines proved very effective. The 1972 convention was indeed peopled mainly with new enthusiasts for candidates and issues rather than old party hands. Only 11 percent of the delegates were repeaters from 1968, and only 15 percent had ever been delegates to *any* previous national convention. In 1968, a total of 102 Democratic members of Congress were delegates; but in 1972 only 58 made the grade. Also in 1972 only 19 of the 30 Democratic governors were delegates, only 13 percent of the delegates belonged to labor unions, and most who did were members of unions not affiliated with the AFL-CIO.[19] But the 1972 delegates represented certain demographic characteristics far more accurately than ever before, as is shown in Table 5.

The new-enthusiast look of the delegates was best captured in a comment by movie actress and delegate Shirley MacLaine—though she herself was untypical for, among other reasons, having been a delegate to the 1968 convention. Her own California delegation, she said with delight, looked "like a couple of high schools, a grape boycott, a

[17] *Mandate for Reform*, pp. 9-13.

[18] For example, Guideline A-5 requires easy access to all the party rules affecting delegate selection; B-1 prohibits proxy voting; B-5 outlaws the unit rule at all stages of the selection process; C-1 requires adequate public notice of all party meetings relevant to the process; C-2 outlaws all ex officio delegates; C-4 prohibits any part of the selection process being held prior to the year of the convention; C-5 limits the number of delegates that can be picked by party committees to 10 percent of the whole; and C-6 urges open access to all slatemaking procedures for particular candidates: *Mandate for Reform*, pp. 41-48.

[19] New York *Times*, July 9, 1972, pp. 1, 33. The data on union membership were provided by the McGovern-Fraser commission staff.

TABLE 5
DEMOGRAPHIC REPRESENTATION IN DEMOCRATIC
NATIONAL CONVENTIONS
(in percent)

		Convention Delegates	
Categories	General Population, 1970	1968	1972
Blacks	11	5	15
Whites	89	95	85
	100	100	100
Women	51	13	40
Men	49	87	60
	100	100	100
Age 18 to 30	27	4	21
Over 30	73	96	79
	100	100	100

Sources: Data for the general population are taken from the *Statistical Abstract of the United States, 1971* (Washington, D.C.: Bureau of the Census, 1971); data for the 1968 convention are taken from *Mandate for Reform* (Washington, D.C.: Democratic National Committee, 1970), pp. 26–29; data for the 3,194 delegates finally seated at the 1972 Convention were furnished by the McGovern-Fraser commission staff.

Black Panther rally, and four or five politicians who walked in the wrong door."[20]

So it must have seemed to most who watched the convention from the galleries or on television. Moreover, the delegates not only looked different from the way most ordinary Democratic voters look, but they also had a different ideological coloring. A survey by the Washington *Post* found that over half of the delegates called themselves "liberal" or "very liberal," compared with the Gallup Poll's finding that only a third of the self-identified Democrats in the general population call themselves any kind of liberal. And only 6.5 percent of the delegates called them-

[20] Quoted in Penn Kemble and Josh Muravchik, "The New Politics & the Democrats," *Commentary*, December, 1972, p. 83.

selves "conservative" or "very conservative," compared with 29 percent of the Democrats in Gallup's sample.

But the delegates' sartorial, tonsorial, and ideological styles may have diverted attention from their predominantly upper-middle-class socioeconomic status. The *Post* survey found that 62 percent of them had annual incomes of over $15,000, compared with 23 percent of the general population. And 39 percent held postgraduate college degrees, compared with only 4 percent of the general population.[21]

These facts should not surprise any student of amateur political activists. Studies of the extralegal party "club" movements in California, New York, and Wisconsin show that they are composed almost entirely of upper-middle-class, college-educated professionals and executives who are motivated mainly by policy commitments rather than by a desire for public office or patronage.[22] This was also the case with the La Follette Progressives. Richard Hofstadter has established that the reform movement was manned largely by middle-class, "old settler," Yankee-Protestant lawyers, teachers, doctors, and small businessmen.[23] He makes a convincing case that this explains why the Progressives' political morality was so different from that of the European immigrants who sustained the big city machines. In one of his most illuminating passages,

[21] Washington *Post*, July 8, 1972, pp. A1, A7.

[22] For the California "clubs," see Francis M. Carney, *The Rise of the Democratic Clubs in California* (New York: Holt, Rinehart and Winston, 1958); James Q. Wilson, *The Amateur Democrats* (Chicago: University of Chicago Press, 1962); and Joseph P. Harris, *California Politics* (San Francisco: Chandler, 1967), Ch. 2. For New York, see Donald C. Blaisdell, "The Riverside Democrats," in Paul Tillett (ed.), *Cases on Party Organization* (New York: McGraw-Hill, 1963), pp. 64-92; and Daniel P. Moynihan, "'Bosses' and 'Reforms': A Profile of New York Democrats," *Commentary*, June, 1961, pp. 461-470. For Wisconsin, see Leon D. Epstein, *Politics in Wisconsin* (Madison, Wis.: University of Wisconsin Press, 1958), Ch. 5; and Frank J. Sorauf, "Extra-Legal Parties in Wisconsin," *American Political Science Review*, 48 (September, 1954), 692-704.

Putting the Right People in Charge

Hofstadter says that the Progressive system of political ethics was

> founded upon the indigenous Yankee-Protestant political traditions, and upon middle-class life, assumed and demanded the constant, disinterested activity of the citizen in public affairs, argued that political life ought to be run, to a greater degree than it was, in accordance with general principles and abstract laws apart from. . . .personal needs, and expressed a common feeling that government should be in good part an effort to moralize the lives of individuals while economic life should be intimately related to the stimulation and development of individual character. The other system, founded upon the European backgrounds of the immigrants, upon their unfamiliarity with independent political action, their familiarity with hierarchy and authority, and upon the urgent needs that so often grew out of their migration, took for granted that the political life of the individual would arise out of family needs, interpreted political and civic relations chiefly in terms of personal obligations, and placed strong personal loyalties above allegiance to abstract codes of law or morals. It was chiefly upon this system of values that the political life of the immigrant, the boss, and the urban machine was based.[24]

Hofstadter adds the somewhat unsettling observation that some of the most influential Progressives acted from

[23] Richard Hofstadter, *The Age of Reform* (New York: Vintage Books, 1955), Chs. IV-V. Roger E. Wyman has shown that the voters who supported the Progressives were much more working-class; but this is not inconsistent with Hofstadter's depiction of the *leaders* as middle-class WASPS: Wyman, "Middle-Class Voters and Progressive Reform: The Conflict of Class and Culture," *American Political Science Review*, 68 (June, 1974), 488-504.

[24] *The Age of Reform*, p. 9.

a mixture of motives that might be encapsulated in the phrase, "What is good for the nation is good for social scientists, and vice-versa." He even singles out a particular set of social scientists:

If the professors had motives of their own for social resentment, the social scientists among them had special reason for a positive interest in the reform movements. The development of regulative and humane legislation required the skills of lawyers and economists, sociologists and political scientists, in the writing of laws and in the staffing of administrative and regulative bodies. Controversy over such issues created a new market for the books and magazine articles of the experts and engendered a new respect for their specialized knowlege. Reform brought with it the brain trust. In Wisconsin even before the turn of the century there was an intimate union between the La Follette regime and the state university at Madison that foreshadowed all later brain trusts.[25]

But in all fairness it should be added that Madison's students as well as its social science professors had a hand in Progressive agitation. We have La Follette's own testimony that:

From the very beginning of our contest we had not only the support of practically all university men throughout the state, but of substantially all of the students of the university old enough to be interested. The spirit of democracy pervaded university life, and a strong body of these fine, clean, brainy fellows—really able men—have been conspicuous in all the Progressive fights of Wisconsin from that day to this.[26]

[25] *Ibid.*, p. 155.

[26] Robert M. La Follette, *La Follette's Autobiography* (Madison, Wis.: Robert M. La Follette Company, 1913), pp. 207-208.

Be that as it may, the only two Ph.D.'s ever to run for President on a major party's ticket were Woodrow Wilson and George McGovern. It might be noted that the political scientist won and the historian lost. But it must be pointed out that the historian achieved his nomination largely because his dedicated and superbly organized band of enthusiasts dominated a convention attended by fewer party regulars than any in history.

Even before the 1972 Convention, some members of the Democrat's two reform commissions felt that the McGovern-Fraser guidelines went too far in discouraging participation by the party's notables. It happened that these particular commissioners had the greatest interest in and influence on the writing of the proposed new charter for the national party. Hence the document sought to reserve at least some guaranteed places for the party's leading officeholders. For example, Article II proposed ex officio membership in the National Party Conferences for all the party's governors and congressmen and for its highest leaders in each house of each state legislature. Article III established ex officio membership on the National Committee for every state party's chairman and highest elected party officer of the opposite sex from the chairman. Seats were also guaranteed for seven members of Congress, four members of the Conference of Democratic Governors, and the member of the National Membership and Finance Council for each state. Article IV reserved places on the National Executive Committee for the highest ranking Democratic leader in the Senate house.[27]

Thus the proposed charter was, in part, an effort to compromise the two competing ideals of who should run the party's affairs. Like many compromises, it drew heavy

[27] The proposed "Charter of the Democratic Party of the United States" is summarized in *Congressional Quarterly Weekly Report*, July 1, 1972, p. 1576.

fire from both sides. Its provisions that the parties' national agencies would continue to consist mainly of persons chosen by state and local conventions of amateur enthusiasts were attacked by most spokesmen for organized labor and the party regulars because they would "permanently establish the rule of the kooks." But the "kooks" also vehemently opposed the charter because it guaranteed some slots for "the party hacks, the bosses, and the fat cats." So the charter's friends decided to settle for the immediate restructuring of the National Committee and the referral of the rest of the proposals to a special commission for review and recommendations to be presented to the 1974 Conference on Democratic Party Organization and Policy.[28]

At the present writing the fate of the proposed charter has yet to be determined; but there is every reason to believe it will be settled mainly in the context of this old and continuing conflict between the party-regular and the enthusiast conception of party membership. It will be mainly a fight inside the national party. However, the laws regulating the state and local parties embody conceptions quite different from either of the two we have just reviewed, and they deserve at least as much attention.

3. *Self-Designated Adherents.* From the 1790s until just after the Civil War, American political parties in most localities were clearly of Duverger's "cadre" type. They neither had nor felt any need for formal rules controlling who could attend local caucuses and be elected to state and national conventions. Any citizen who felt like showing up at a local caucus did, and there are few recorded instances of Federalists or Whigs trying to "raid" Republican or Democratic meetings. The numbers of activists in

[28] The conflict and compromise over the proposed charter are described in *Congressional Quarterly Weekly Report*, July 15, 1972, p. 1777.

both parties in most places were so small that everyone knew everyone else, and "raiding" was simply not feasible.[29]

Things began to change after the Civil War, when, as we observed in Chapter 3, the states began to adopt laws regulating parties. Some of these early laws laid down legal qualifications for the right to participate in party caucuses and conventions. Most required the would-be participant to take some kind of oath: for example, that he had not voted against, or had voted for, the party's candidates in the preceding election (as in Wisconsin and Minnesota); or that he was a member of the party and would support its "aims and objects" (as in Michigan); or that he was not a member of any other party (as in Massachusetts).[30]

However, from 1903 on most states adopted comprehensive and mandatory direct primary laws, and were thus forced to adopt rules governing who could vote in a particular party's primary. A few followed Wisconsin's lead in choosing "open" primaries, but most established and still have "closed" primaries—that is, primaries legally closed to all but the party's "members." Each of these states needed and adopted a legal definition of the qualifications for party membership.

The closed-primary states have since chosen many different definitions,[31] but all have been variations on a few basic themes. The party member must be a registered voter; he must satisfy some test of his good-faith membership in the party by attesting to either his past allegiance, his present affiliation, or his intended future allegiance.

[29] Cf. Luetscher, *op. cit.*, pp. 66-67.
[30] The early legal requirements are summarized in Charles E. Merriam, *Primary Elections* (Chicago: University of Chicago Press, 1908), pp. 36-38.
[31] The most comprehensive survey of the states' legal definitions of party membership is Clarence A. Berdahl, "Party Membership in the United States," *American Political Science Review*, 36 (February, April, 1942), 16-50, 241-262.

And in most states these tests are presumably enforced either by requiring prior registration as a party member or by allowing a party official to challenge the bona fides of anyone suspected of attempting to "raid" its primary.

But there is no point in reviewing the details of these "tests" and "enforcement methods," for they are all more or less meaningless in practice. Each state's election laws strictly preserve secrecy about what parties and candidates the voter actually votes for in general elections, and so there is no practical way to check the validity of the voter's declaration of his past allegiance or future intentions. Registration officials and courts have no realistic alternative to taking the voter's word for it, and as a result the "challenge" provisions of the primary laws are almost never used.

Moreover, even these feeble requirements for party membership have been challenged in the federal courts recently, and their present status is shaky at best. One set of cases involved two provisions of the Illinois primary law. The first prohibited a person from running as a candidate in one party's primary if he had voted in another party's primary within the preceding twenty-three months. The second provided that each voter would receive whichever party's primary ballot he requested unless he had voted in another party's primary within the same period. Since the primaries for all national and most state and local offices were held every twenty-*four* months, these restrictions were less than Draconian in their severity. Their only effect has been to keep the handful of persons who voted or ran in one party's primary for municipal offices in odd-numbered years from voting and running in the other party's primary in the even-numbered year immediately following.

Nevertheless, the constitutionality of both restrictions has been challenged. In 1971 a federal district court unanimously upheld the constitutionality of the twenty-three month rule for *candidates*, on the ground that the state had a "compelling interest" in preserving the integrity of the two-party system by preventing candidates from casually switching parties. But the court added the significant dictum that the restriction on *voters* might well be a different matter:

> The state's interest in preserving a vigorous and competitive two-party system is fostered by the requirement that candidates demonstrate a certain loyalty and attachment to the party in whose primary they are running; the same cannot be said of voters, however, *who should be freer to demonstrate their changes in political attitude by voting for popular candidates or against unpopular candidates in any party's primary election.* Thus, it is not inconsistent to prevent candidates from switching parties from election to election and at the same time to permit voters to do so.[32]

In 1973 the Supreme Court turned this dictum into a rule of law. They voted by 7 to 2 that the twenty-three month rule for *voters* was unconstitutional. *Any* restriction on a voter's freedom to vote in any election, primary or general, can be justified, the majority said, only by a compelling state interest; and in this case the state interest was not sufficiently compelling to overcome the voter's freedom. In the majority's words:

> Under our political system, a basic function of a political party is to select the candidates for public office to be offered to the voters at general elections.

[32] *Bendinger v. Ogilvie*, 335 F. Supp. 572 (1971) at 576, emphasis added.

A prime objective of most voters in associating themselves with a particular party must surely be to gain
a voice in that selection process. By preventing the
appellee from participating at all in Democratic primary elections during the statutory period, the Illinois
statute deprived her of any voice in choosing the
party's candidates, and thus substantially abridged
her ability to associate effectively with the party of
her choice.[33]

The logical extension of the 1971 dictum and the 1973
ruling is that every voter has the constitutional right to
vote for candidates for every office in *both* parties' primaries every time they are held. If and when that becomes
law, the concept of party membership will become meaningless in America, and Jefferson's pious hope, expressed
in his 1801 inaugural address, will become legal fact: we
will indeed all be Democrats and all be Republicans.

In 1973, however, the Supreme Court—by the narrowest
of margins—refused to go the final step. It reviewed the
provision in New York's primary law that a voter must
register in the party of his choice at least 30 days prior
to a general election in order to be eligible to vote in that
party's primary held *after* the general election. This means,
in effect, that the voter must register with a party from
eight to eleven months prior to voting in its primary,
although he can also change his party registration for each
primary if he cares to do so. The Court of Appeals upheld
this rule as a legitimate device for serving the compelling
state interest in preventing raiding. The Supreme Court
agreed, but only by a bare 5 to 4 majority.

The New York decisions mean that, for the moment
at least, *some* cutoff period for party registration prior
to a primary is constitutionally permissible. But they also

[33] *Kusper v. Pontikes*, 94 S. Ct. 303 (1973) at 308.

dramatized how differently different federal judges balance the competing values of preserving the parties' integrity as against allowing the voters freedom to vote in any and all party primaries they wish. The two principal views are worth quoting.

Thus the Court of Appeals said in upholding the New York law:

> The political parties in the United States, though broadbased enough so that their members' philosophies often range across the political spectrum, stand as deliberate associations of individuals drawn together to advance certain common aims by nominating and electing candidates who will pursue those aims once in office. The entire political process depends largely upon the satisfactory operation of these institutions. . . .Yet the efficacy of the party system in the democratic process—its usefulness in providing a unity of divergent factions in an alliance for power—would be seriously impaired were members of one party entitled to interfere and participate in the other party's affairs. In such circumstances, the raided party would be hardpressed to put forth the candidates its members deemed most satisfactory. In the end the chief loser would be the public.[34]

Five Supreme Court justices expressed their agreement with this view, but four agreed with the quite different view of party membership and its importance expressed in Justice Powell's dissenting opinion:

> Political parties in this country traditionally have been characterized by a fluidity and overlap of philosophy and membership. And citizens generally declare

[34] *Rosario v. Rockefeller*, 458 F. 2d. 649 (1972) at 652.

or alter party affiliation for reasons quite unconnected with any premeditated intention to disrupt or frustrate the plans of a party with which they are not in sympathy. Citizens customarily choose a party and vote in the primary simply because it presents candidates and issues more responsive to their immediate concerns and aspirations. . . .That a citizen should be absolutely precluded so far in advance from voting in a party primary in response to a sympathetic candidate, a new or meaningful issue, or changing party philosophies in his State, runs contrary to the fundamental rights of personal choice and expression which voting in this country was designed to serve.[35]

So the constitutional status of primary laws restricting voters from switching parties whenever they wish remains very much in doubt, and there is no reason to suppose that the 1973 decisions preserve them forever. But whatever may be the future of such laws, the essence of the legal definitions of party membership in the United States will surely continue to be *self-designation*. The fact remains that today even in Illinois, New York, or any other closed-primary state you are a Democrat if you say you are; no one can effectively say you are not; and you can become a Republican any time the spirit moves you simply by saying that you have become one. You accept no obligations by such a declaration; you receive only a privilege—the privilege of taking an equal part in the making of the party's most important decision, the nomination of its candidates for public office. The only remaining restriction is that in some states, such as California, you may have to let the registrar of voters know that you have changed parties, and you may have to do so several

[35] *Rosario v. Rockefeller*, 93 S. Ct. 1245 (1973) at 1256.

weeks or even months before your new party's next primary. But in many closed-primary states you do not even have to do that, and in Wisconsin and the other open-primary states you are not *allowed* to make an official declaration of your party membership membership. One can only conclude that the so-called "closed" primaries are just a hair more closed than the so-called "open" primaries.

4. *Any and All Voters.* Despite the almost total ineffectiveness of their tests and methods of enforcement, the closed-primary states at least retain some vestiges of the idea that only Democrats should vote in Democratic primaries and only Republicans in Republican primaries. And, as we noted in Chapter 3, the 1972 Democratic National Convention tried to reaffirm this principle by ordering that in 1976 no delegates shall be seated who have been elected in primaries where "crossover" voting is allowed.

Many Americans, however, have felt that even requiring a voter to publicly declare his party affiliation as a precondition for voting in a primary is unjust, for it makes him vulnerable to reprisals by employers and neighbors who support the other party. For example, John R. Commons, who was one of those Wisconsin social scientists Hofstadter talks about, spoke for many of his fellow Progressives, then and now, when he declared:

> now that the official ballot is secret, so that a voter's declaration and oath of [party] affiliation at the primary are not binding, it would seem to be the true interest of the parties in framing a primary election law in order to protect themselves from nominations by voters under duress, to make the primary also secret. This could be done by a blanket ballot contain-

ing the names of all candidates for nomination by all parties, and by dispensing with all declarations or oaths of party affiliation.[36]

Anyone who thinks Commons' views are quaint or archaic should be reminded that at present two states, Alaska and Washington, conduct their primaries exactly as Commons wished, and seven more (Michigan, Minnesota, Montana, North Dakota, Utah, Vermont, and Wisconsin) allow their voters to vote in either party's primary, though not both, whenever they wish.[37] Furthermore, the political culture that supports open primaries is far from dead, at least in Wisconsin. We learned this in 1966 when we asked a sample of Wisconsin adults whether they thought the state should change to a closed primary. Only 9 percent said yes, and a whopping 82 percent said no. When asked why they felt that way, 31 percent replied that one should always vote for the man and not the party; and 36 percent said the open primary guarantees freedom of voting for everyone by allowing independents to vote in primaries and partisans to change their minds.[38] But in the characteristic American mode of thinking about these matters, they were not *entirely* antiparty: only 34 percent agreed with the statement that "It would be better if, in all elections, no party labels were put on the ballots," while 56 percent disagreed.

Whatever may be the merits of the four conflicting American conceptions of party membership, a few factual observations can be made. The self-designation view dominates most state and local parties through the wide use

[36] John R. Commons, address published in *Proceedings of the National Conference on Practical Reform of Primary Elections, January 20-21, 1898* (Chicago: Wm. C. Hollister & Bro., 1898), p. 22.

[37] *The Book of the States, 1972-1973* (Lexington, Ky.: Council of State Governments, 1972), table on p. 29.

[38] Data collected by the Survey Research Laboratory of the University of Wisconsin, Project 266 (Winter, 1966), Deck 01, question 8.

of the closed primary. Its only serious rival at these levels is the all-voters view, which prevails in the open-primary states. At the national level the party-regulars view prevailed most of the time from the 1790s to the 1960s. Since 1968, however, it has been largely overtaken in both parties by the occasional-enthusiasts conception; and if any of the current proposals for a national presidential primary become law, the self-designation view or the any-voter view will govern most national party affairs as well.

No matter what the outcome, the dispute over who should and should not be treated as a party member will continue to be one of the most basic of all of the issues in disputes over party reform. For one's position on that issue largely determines one's views about whom the parties' representative agencies should represent, about whose candidate and issue preferences they should respond to, and about how things need to be arranged in order to put the right people in charge. And that, as we have seen, is what most conflict over party reform in America ultimately comes down to.[39]

But issues of putting the right people in charge have also been central in another significant arena of party reform: the perennial struggle between national and subnational party agencies over the rightful location of their parties' ultimate decision-making powers. In my judgment, some of the most significant—and least noticed—changes in both parties in recent decades have come in this arena. Their story deserves more attention than most party-watchers have given it, and its main outlines are our next concern.

NATIONAL VERSUS LOCAL CONTROL

Leon Epstein's survey of Western-style parties succinctly states a basic truth about their organizational structures:

[39] For an exposition of this point by a strong adherent of the

Just as political parties have been functional responses to voting by a mass electorate, so their nongovernmental or extra-parliamentary organizations have been means created by party leaders, including candidates, to help win votes and secure office. Organization in one degree or another always exists for this electoral purpose. It may have other purposes as well and still be regarded as that of a party, provided the electoral purpose is prominent, if not dominant.[40]

As a result, almost all parties in Western democracies tie their organizations to the nations' election structures: for each level of government with significant elective offices, the parties establish a level of organization to nominate candidates and contest elections for those offices.

Accordingly, since most Western nations have elections for major subnational offices as well as for national offices, their parties typically have not only national organizations but constituency and regional or provincial organizations as well. The various levels usually develop different interests, and so in most Western parties conflict is endemic between the national and subnational agencies over such critical matters as selection of candidates, formulation of programs, allocation of funds, and enactment of party rules.[41]

American parties certainly constitute a leading case in point. Throughout our history many of the fights over

party-regular view, see E.E. Schattschneider, *Party Government* (New York: Farrar and Rinehart, 1942), pp. 53-61.

[40] Epstein, *Political Parties in Western Democracies*, p. 98.

[41] The illustrations are endless, but a sample includes: *ibid.*, pp. 216-218; Duverger, *op. cit.*, pp. 40-62; Austin Ranney, *Pathways to Parliament* (Madison, Wis.: University of Wisconsin Press, 1965), pp. 42-56, 154-166; Henry Valen and Daniel Katz, *Political Parties in Norway* (Oslo: Universitetsforlaget, 1964), pp. 87-92; and Jeffrey Obler, "The Role of National Party Leaders in the Selection of Parliamentary Candidates: The Belgian Case," *Comparative Politics*, 5 (January 1973), 157-184.

party reform have involved conflict over the relative powers of the national and state parties. The story falls into two main periods. The first, from 1824 to 1956, saw the steady aggrandizement of the state organizations at the expense of the national agencies, with the result that our national parties became by far the weakest in the Western world. In the second period, from 1956 to the present, the national party committees and conventions have substantially reversed this trend by reacquiring the power to control their own affairs. We shall examine each period in detail.

THE DECLINE OF THE NATIONAL PARTIES, 1824 TO 1956

1. *Abolition of the Congressional Caucus.* It is well to remember that during its heyday from 1800 to 1824 the congressional caucus was a highly centralized national party agency making the original Republican party's most important single decision: the choice of its presidential candidate. Many of its enemies, as we have seen, attacked the caucus mainly on the ground that it was unrepresentative and undemocratic. But one of the most effective criticisms was the charge that the caucus, by overbearing the powers of state parties, was effectively abridging the constitutional rights of states. Thus Senator Rufus King argued in 1824 that "this central junto" had the power and the inclination to subvert the sovereignty of the states. If it continued, he warned,

> it will eventually lead to the total destruction of the rights of the small States, and that clause in the Constitution which secures their just weight in the choice of a President, will be virtually repealed.[42]

[42] Speech to the Senate, March 18, 1824, quoted in Thomas Hart Benton (ed.), *Abridgment of the Debates of Congress, from 1789 to*

This argument played no small part in the overthrow of the caucus. As we have seen, it was stripped of its presidential nominating function in the period from 1824 to 1828 mainly by the efforts of Andrew Jackson's coalition of regulars and enthusiasts. Jackson, though a United States Senator, had never been a member of the congressional "club" of his time, and his candidacy was in good measure an effort by local and state party leaders to end the domination of presidential politics by the only significant national party agency of the time. Hence in 1824 and again in 1828 Jackson's name was put forth by various state legislatures and state legislative caucuses, and many of his supporters among the state and local parties vowed that, once the national caucus had been overthrown in Jackson's interest, presidential nominations should always thereafter be made in the same highly decentralized fashion.[43] Things did not work out quite that way, but Schattschneider accurately sums up the significance of Jackson's triumph:

> the fall of the congressional caucus in the 1820s is one of the most important events in American history. It marks a great collapse of the authority of the central party group. Until 1824, the power to nominate a party candidate for the presidency was firmly in the hands of the national party leaders. ... Invariably the nominee had long been prominent in national politics, was a leading member of the group in control

1856 (New York: D. Appleton, 1859), Vol. VII, p. 526. For other expressions of this view, see Robert V. Remini, *Martin Van Buren and the Making of the Democratic Party* (New York: Columbia University Press, 1959), pp. 47-49.

[43] Cf. M.I. Ostrogorski, *Democracy and the Organization of Political Parties*, translated from the French by Frederick Clarke (New York: Macmillan, 1902), Vol. II, pp. 40-41, and Edgar E. Robinson, *The Evolution of American Political Parties* (New York: Harcourt, Brace, 1924), p. 102.

of the politics of the capital; with one exception he was first Secretary of State, then became a candidate for the presidency. Thus there was a recognized career leading to the presidency, and men were marked for the presidency well in advance. The road to glory was monopolized by the national party leaders. It is noteworthy that this process was noiseless and decorous, i.e., the decisions were made privately within the ranks of the national leadership. The election of Andrew Jackson, the first rank outsider to make a successful raid on the national party leadership, marks the breakdown of the system.[44]

Schattschneider's portrayal of how the congressional caucus chose presidential candidates looks remarkably like Robert McKenzie's classic description of how British parliamentary parties have chosen their leaders and thus the nation's prime ministers.[45] This resemblance illuminates Theodore Lowi's perceptive conclusion that the fall of the caucus not only altered the character of the parties but changed the constitutional system as well. He points out that from 1790 to the 1820s the main impact of caucus nominations was to convert the formal separation of powers between the President and Congress into a de facto "fusion of powers" not unlike such modern parliamentary systems as the British. But the end of the caucus and the rise of Jackson and presidential nominations by national conventions composed of delegations from state parties gave "him and succeeding Presidents a base of power independent of Congress. . . .totally split Congress off from the presidential succession, and established, for the first time, an institutionalized, *real* separation of

[44] Schattschneider, *op. cit.*, p. 152.
[45] Robert McKenzie, *British Political Parties* (2d ed., London: Mercury Books, 1963), Chs. II-III, VI-VII, X-XI.

powers."[46] Perhaps this episode is enough by itself to establish the point that party reforms can have profound effects upon the larger political system.

2. *Organizing the National Conventions.* The state and local party leaders thus won a great victory in ending presidential nominations by congressional caucus. To be sure, the political necessities created by the revival of national two-party competition soon made them abandon nominations by state legislatures and legislative caucuses for a more effective unifying device. But in organizing the new national conventions for this purpose in the early 1830s they had no intention of reviving party centralization, and in the first conventions they adopted three major rules designed to prevent it.

First, the precedent was firmly established that, while the convention would decide how many votes each state party would have at the next convention, the state parties would have sole control over how the delegates casting those votes would be chosen. This principle remained unchallenged for well over a century and played a major role in making the conventions what they were.[47]

Second, the Democratic and Whig conventions left it up to each state delegation to decide whether or not it would use the "unit rule," which required that each delegation's *entire* vote be cast as its majority directed. If the delegation or its state committee elected to use the rule to maximize the unity and power of its votes, the convention would enforce it. The new Republican party founded in 1854 had a different rule. Since they formed

[46] Theodore J. Lowi, "Party, Policy, and Constitution in America," in William Nisbet Chambers and Walter Dean Burnham (eds.), *The American Party Systems* (New York: Oxford University Press, 1967), p. 248, emphasis in the original.

[47] Paul T. David, Ralph M. Goldman, and Richard C. Bain, *The Politics of National Party Conventions* (Washington, D.C.: Brookings Institution, 1960), pp. 18, 165.

their party to defend national supremacy against the doctrines of states' rights and secession, the rule made no sense to them. So they rejected it at their first national convention in 1856 and have never used it. Their action touched off a few sporadic efforts in Democratic conventions to repeal the rule, but none succeeded until 1968. The basic argument which preserved the rule for so long was forthrightly stated in the Democratic convention of 1884 by a delegate from, appropriately, Wisconsin:

> I know, Mr. President, that in the Republican party—a party which believes that Congress and the Federal Government have every power which is not expressly denied, and that the states have hardly any rights left which the Federal Government is bound to respect—they can adopt in their convention this idea that a state does not control its own delegation in a national convention. Not so in the convention of the great Democratic party. We stand, Mr. President, for the rights of the States.[48]

Third, in their first convention in 1832 the Democrats adopted the rule that both the presidential and vice-presidential nominations required the support of two-thirds of the delegates voting. The rule was originally said to ensure that the nomination would have the greatest possible support from all sections of the country, but the main justification for it soon became that it prevented a few large states from using the unit rule to control the nominations. Since at each succeeding convention the two-thirds rule was adopted, along with the other rules, by simple majorities and was therefore repealable by simple majori-

[48] Quoted in Carl Becker, "The Unit Rule in National Nominating Conventions," *American Historical Review*, 5 (October 1899), 64-82, p. 82. See also David, Goldman, and Bain, *op. cit.*, pp. 199-203.

ties, it should have been as easy to drop as any other rule. Several efforts were made to repeal it, but none succeeded until 1936, when the powerful forces led by Franklin Delano Roosevelt insisted that the party had become a truly national party and no longer needed special rules to protect the interests of the South or any other aggregation of states.[49] So until well into the twentieth century the national conventions remained gatherings that, in the view of some observers, resembled nothing so much as "international conferences of delegates from sovereign nations."[50]

3. *Apportioning the National Committees.* The establishment of the first national committee by the Democrats in 1848 could have started renationalizing the parties, but it did not.[51] In 1845 Congress passed a new law requiring that all presidential electors be chosen on the same day, not, as heretofore, when each state decided to do so. Many party leaders felt this change necessitated some better way of coordinating presidential campaigns; for up to that time the practice had been to leave it up to each state party to decide its own campaign strategy and scheduling. The argument seemed persuasive to most of the 1848 Democratic convention's delegates, and they adopted the following motion:

> Ordered, that a committee of *one from each state, to be named by the respective delegations*, be appointed to promote the Democratic cause, with power to fill vacancies, and to be designated "The Democratic National Committee."[52]

[49] David, Goldman, and Bain, *op. cit.*, pp. 208-213.

[50] *Ibid.*, p. 2.

[51] The most complete account is Cornelius P. Cotter and Bernard C. Hennessy, *Politics Without Power: The National Party Committees* (New York: Atherton Press, 1964), pp. 13-16, 20-22. See also Hugh A. Bone, *Party Committees and National Politics* (Seattle, Wash.: University of Washington Press, 1958), Ch. 1.

[52] Quoted in Cotter and Hennessy, *op. cit.*, p. 14, emphasis added.

Putting the Right People in Charge

Note that in establishing a national committee the Democrats established several precedents guaranteeing that it would be little, if any, more centralizing than the national conventions. First, they departed from the national convention's electoral-college apportionment formula and chose instead to give each state equal representation. This was not done in a fit of absent-mindedness. The original motion provided for a committee of fifteen members, all to be chosen by the convention chairman. But a number of the smaller Western states feared that such a committee would be dominated by the older, more populous states. So, led by Senator Jesse D. Bright of Indiana, they persuaded the convention to accept an amendment providing for one member from each state. And second, the convention also established the principle that the members of the national committee would be appointed by each state's delegation and accepted by the committee without question. The Republicans followed both precedents in establishing their own committee eight years later, and what might have been a triumph for the national parties turned out to be another of a long string of victories for the state and local parties. In 1920 both parties added a national committeewoman for each state, but this left unchanged the committee's highly decentralized apportionment and selection rules, which continued in force until the 1950s.

4. *Direct Primary Nominations of U.S. Senators and Representatives.* Many political parties in other Western democracies have some formal procedure by which their national agencies can veto the candidacies of unacceptable persons chosen by their local subdivisions. At first glance this seems to American eyes the very zenith of centralized party power, but a second glance shows that things are not quite as simple as they seem. A number of recent studies have shown that in practice the central veto power

is used rarely or never, and that it plays, at most, a minor role in keeping public officeholders faithful to their parties' programs.[53]

However, weak the central veto power may be in other parties, it has long been nonexistent in American parties. Even in the nineteenth century there is little evidence of any efforts—let alone successful ones—by national leaders to influence local nominations for congressional candidates. The traditional local control of nominations was nailed down even more firmly by the states' general adoption of direct primary nominations after 1903. Since then a few Presidents[54] have tried to "purge" maverick congressmen of their parties by urging their defeat in state and district primaries. But most such efforts have failed utterly, and the few exceptions have all come in cases where the *local* organizations have worked to dump the incumbent for their own reasons.[55] Even more significant, most national as well as state and local party leaders have condemned the morality of attempts at national "purges." One of the most striking statements of this view was made by James A. Farley, one of the most powerful national party chairmen in history. Though a longtime supporter of Franklin Roosevelt, he wrote of his chief's unsuccessful effort to "purge" thirteen anti-New Deal Democrats in the 1938 primaries:

[53] This is certainly the case in Great Britain, where the formal veto power *appears* to be most formidable: see Austin Ranney, "Candidate Selection and Party Cohesion in Britain and the United States," in William J. Crotty, Donald M. Freeman, and Douglas S. Gatlin (eds.), *Political Parties and Political Behavior* (2d ed., Boston: Allyn and Bacon, 1971), pp. 248-264. For other Western nations, see the studies reviewed in Epstein, *Political Parties in Western Democracies*, Ch. 8, and Obler, *op. cit.*, fn. 5, pp. 159-160.

[54] Notably Taft in 1910, Wilson in 1918, Truman in 1946, and, above all, Roosevelt in 1938.

[55] These efforts at "purges" and their fates are reviewed in Austin Ranney and Willmoore Kendall, *Democracy and the American Party System* (New York: Harcourt, Brace, 1956), pp. 286-289. See also V.O.

Putting the Right People in Charge

I knew from the beginning that the purge could lead to nothing but misfortune, because in pursuing his course of vengeance Roosevelt violated a cardinal political creed which demanded that he keep out of local matters. Sound doctrine is sound politics. When Roosevelt began neglecting the rules of the game, I lost faith in him. I trace all the woes of the Democratic party, directly or indirectly, to this interference in purely local affairs. In any political entity voters naturally and rightfully resent the unwarranted invasion of outsiders.[56]

Now when a powerful national party chairman describes his President's efforts to prevent the renomination of congressmen working against the national party program as "the unwarranted invasion of outsiders" and as "interference in purely local affairs," we can well understand the judgment of most political scientists that the net result of party development from 1824 to the 1950s was to make American parties the least centralized in the world. Schattschneider put the point with characteristic pungence in his assertions published in 1942 that the national party agencies were "only the transparent filaments of the ghost of a party" and that "decentralization is by all odds the most important single characteristic of the American major party."[57] Schattschneider's language may seem a bit strong, but most analysts agree with Frank Sorauf's later comment that "closer examination of the American parties reveals that what seems to be hyperbole is merely bald statement of reality."[58]

Key, Jr., *Politics, Parties & Pressure Groups* (5th ed., New York: Thomas Y. Crowell, 1964), pp. 442-446.

[56] *Jim Farley's Story: The Roosevelt Years* (New York: McGraw-Hill, 1948), pp. 146-147.

[57] Schattschneider, *op. cit.*, pp. 163, 129.

[58] Frank J. Sorauf, *Party Politics in America* (2d ed., Boston: Little, Brown, 1972), p. 113. For other recent statements of this view, see

Curing the Mischiefs of Faction

I do not question the essential accuracy of these judgments, but I do believe that since the 1950s there has taken place, mainly but not entirely in the Democratic party, a modest but distinct revival of national party control. Surprisingly little attention has been paid to this development, but it has already made a major difference in some matters and may go a good deal further. It therefore seems appropriate to conclude this chapter by briefly describing what has been happening.

THE REVIVAL OF NATIONAL CONTROL, 1956 TO THE PRESENT

1. *The National Committee's Control of Its Own Members.* We noted earlier that for over a century after its establishment in 1848 the Democratic National Committee accepted without question any and all members selected for it by the state parties it was supposed to represent. However, the defections of some Southern Democrats to the Dixiecrats in 1948 and to the Republicans in 1952 led to two episodes which established the National Committee's claim to be the final judge of the qualifications of its own members. They were also the opening moves in an accelerating drive to strengthen national party agencies in general.

The first episode involved Wright Morrow, the National Committeeman from Texas who openly supported the Republican presidential candidate in 1952. He wrote to National Chairman Stephen Mitchell explaining his actions, and Mitchell chose to interpret the letter as Morrow's resignation from the National Committee. Morrow denied any such intent, and he and the Texas State Central Committee insisted that he was still their duly elected National Committeeman whom the National Committee

---

Key, *op. cit.*, pp. 315-316; Polsby and Wildavsky, *op. cit.*, pp. 30-31; and Allan P. Sindler, *Political Parties in the United States* (New York: St. Martin's Press, 1966), pp. 73-74.

were obliged to accept whether they liked him or not. But the Committee backed up Mitchell and treated Morrow's seat as vacant until 1955, when the Texans were persuaded by Lyndon Johnson and Sam Rayburn to appoint a new Committeeman acceptable to the national body.

The second episode took place in 1958 when the State Central Committee of Louisiana voted to remove their National Committeeman, Camille Gravel, Jr., because he was "soft" on questions of racial segregation. National Chairman Paul Butler and the National Committee refused to accept that Gravel was removed or that the successor appointed by the Louisiana party had any claim to the seat. Chairman Butler asserted the new principle in a television interview:

> until the National Committee votes by a two-thirds vote to remove [Gravel] he will remain the representative of the Democratic Party in Louisiana, and we will not recognize the action taken by the State Committee, and that is according to the rules.[59]

The Morrow and Gravel affairs were the first instances in many, many years in which *any* national party agency asserted its right to be the final judge of its own members. The National Committee made it stick, and the principle has since been incorporated in the more significant area of the national conventions.

2. *The National Convention's Control of Its Own Members.* The current revival of national control in the Democratic party was touched off by the deepest schism it has experienced since the 1850s. The full story of the Dixiecrat revolt of 1948 is too long to be retold here,[60]

---

[59] Quoted in Cotter and Hennessy, *op. cit.*, p. 33.
[60] One useful account is Emile P. Ader, *The Dixiecrat Movement* (Washington, D.C.: Public Affairs Press, 1955).

but its consequences for party reform have been considerable. The Dixiecrats' strategic objective was to have their ticket of J. Strom Thurmond and Fielding Wright carry enough Southern states to throw the presidential election into the House of Representatives where they could barter their votes to one or the other major party in return for a commitment to end federal intervention in Southern race relations. They were well aware that Southern voters' ingrained loyalty to the Democratic label would defeat the Thurmond-Wright ticket if it ran as a third party. So their main tactic was to have the Dixiecrat pair listed on the ballots of the Southern states under the regular name and symbols of the Democratic party. It was a shrewd strategy and tactic, but they were able to bring it off in only four states, and these were the only four states they carried.

Most Northern Democrats were outraged, not so much by the Dixiecrats' defection itself as by their effort to steal the Democratic label. At the 1952 national convention they proposed various forms of "loyalty oaths" as preconditions for seating Southern delegates, but they were all referred to a special committee headed by National Chairman Stephen Mitchell. The committee recommended and the 1956 convention adopted a new rule, which was incorporated in the calls for all subsequent conventions:

It is the understanding that a State Democratic Party, in selecting and certifying delegates to the Democratic National Convention, thereby undertakes to assure that voters will have the opportunity to cast their election ballots for the Presidential and Vice-Presidential nominees selected by said Convention, and for electors pledged formally and in good conscience to the election of those Presidential and

Vice-Presidential nominees under the Democratic party label and designation.[61]

This may not have seemed very revolutionary at the time, but it was the first move in the greatest change in the relations between national and state party agencies since the convention replaced the congressional caucus. It established the centralizing principle that henceforth the national party agencies will not only decide how many votes each state delegation gets at the national convention but will also impose national rules on what kinds of persons can be selected.

This new principle was carried one long step further in 1964 when it was extended to include nationally imposed requirements on *how* each state party must select its delegates. Though portrayed by the mass media at the time as merely an ad hoc compromise solution of the conflict over the Mississippi Freedom Democratic Party, the new no-discrimination resolution was in fact a highly significant further extension of the national party's power. It provided that the Call for the 1968 convention and all subsequent conventions would include the following added language in the section entitled "Qualifications of State Delegations":

It is the understanding that a State Democratic Party, in selecting and certifying delegates to the Democratic National Convention, thereby undertakes to assure that voters in the State, regardless of race,

[61] The "loyalty oath" controversy and its consequences are well described in Allan P. Sindler, "The Unsolid South: A Challenge to the Democratic Party," in Alan Westin (ed.), *The Uses of Power* (New York: Harcourt, Brace, 1962); and Abraham Holtzman, "Party Responsibility and Loyalty: New Rules in the Democratic Party," *Journal of Politics*, 22 (1960), 485-501.

color, creed or national origin, will have the opportunity to participate fully in Party affairs. . . .[62]

Furthermore, the rule was no paper tiger. It provided the basis for the decision of the 1968 Credentials Committee, backed up by the Convention, to deny seats to the entire "regular" Mississippi delegation and to seat in their stead the delegation of the Loyal Democrats of Mississippi, which had been selected by nondiscriminatory procedures.

The way was thus further prepared for the sweeping changes made between 1969 and 1972 by the McGovern-Fraser commission and the national committee. In 1969 the committee, acting under a mandate from the 1968 convention, established the Commission on Party Structure and Delegate Selection. Under the chairmanship, first of Senator George McGovern and, after 1971, of Representative Donald Fraser, the commission developed a set of eighteen guidelines governing the state parties' procedures for selecting their delegates to the national conventions. The national committee accepted all the guidelines and declared in the Call for the 1972 convention that they constituted "the standards that State Democratic Parties, in qualifying and certifying delegates to the 1972 Democratic National Convention, must make all efforts to comply with."[63] And they made it stick: forty-five of the fifty-five state and territorial parties were in full compliance with the guidelines by convention time, and the other ten were in substantial compliance.

In Chapter 4 we noted some of the problems created by the guidelines' embracing of several conflicting princi-

[62] Democratic National Committee, *Preliminary Call for the 1968 Democratic National Convention* (Washington, D.C.: Democratic National Committee, 1967), Section II.

[63] Democratic National Committee, *Preliminary Call for the 1972 Democratic National Convention* (Washington, D.C.: Democratic National Committee, 1971), Section II.

ples of representation. But the point to be emphasized here is what they have done to revive the national party agencies' power over their state affiliates. The commission was mandated by a national convention, appointed and encouraged by a national chairman, and given real clout by a national committee. The guidelines required the state parties to make radical changes in many of their accustomed ways of doing things, and the state parties all got into line. The national agencies' only sanction was their power to refuse convention seats to delegates from non-complying state parties; but it proved quite powerful enough.

In 1973 the guidelines were revised by a new commission mandated by the 1972 convention and put into force for the 1976 convention by a decision of the Democratic National Committee.[64] Thus the party's national agencies have reaffirmed their power to govern the state parties' delegate-selection procedures. Taken together, the work of the two commissions constitutes one of the most significant episodes yet in the story of reviving national intraparty power.

3. *The 1972 Convention's Directives.* As we have noted in earlier chapters, the 1972 Democratic National Convention made several of the most sweeping assertions ever made of the superiority of national party rules over state party rules *and state laws*. First, it required that all delegates to the next convention be "chosen in a manner which fairly reflects the division of preferences expressed by those who participate in the Presidential nominating process in each state. . . ."[65] Second, it required that the

[64] The new commission was known as the "Mikulski commission", after its chairwoman, Barbara A. Mikulski: *Democrats All* (Washington, D.C.: Democratic National Committee, 1973). For the DNC's action, see *Congressional Quarterly Weekly Report*, February 9, 1974, pp. 297-300.

[65] *Report of the Committee on Rules to the 1972 Democratic National Convention* (mimeo.), Section 4.

delegates also be "selected through or mandated by Primary elections conducted by public authority or by other selection processes in which adequate provision is made to restrict participation in such elections of processes to ... Democratic voters who have been registered as such ... through a system of state or federal voter registration which includes party registration. ...."[66]

The first rule directs a change in the winner-take-all presidential primary laws of California and South Dakota. The second directs a change in the open presidential primary laws of Michigan and Wisconsin. But what if these states refuse to change their laws? Will the 1976 convention flatly refuse to seat any of their delegates even though they are duly elected by the states' voters according to state laws? The convention drew back from that rather alarming possibility by including an escape clause:

> In the event that state law does not permit a state Party to conform with the provisions of this section, it has an obligation to make *all feasible efforts* to repeal, amend or otherwise modify such laws to accomplish these objectives.[67]

Presumably, then, if the California or Wisconsin Democratic parties try hard, but fail, to get their states' presidential primary laws changed as directed, the 1976 convention will nevertheless seat their delegates. But the directives to change state laws are in themselves substantial extensions of similar provisions in the McGovern-Fraser commission's guidelines.

4. *The Proposed National Party Charter.* It may turn out that the 1972 Democratic convention's most significant acceleration of the movement to increase national party power will be its calling of the 1974 Conference on

[66] *Ibid.*, Section 9, paragraph 1.
[67] *Ibid.*, Section 9, paragraph 3, emphasis added.

Party Organization and Policy. That conference's main task will be to consider and act upon some version of the most radical plan yet proposed to centralize power in a national party: the Charter of the Democratic Party of the United States jointly proposed in 1972 by the O'Hara and McGovern-Fraser commissions. Their charter strengthens the position of the national committee and the national chairman, and it proposes two new agencies— the off-year national policy conferences and the national membership and finance council—intended to make the national party much more active *between* presidential elections. The most far-reaching of all its provisions is the proposal that all national party organs outside Congress except the national conventions be manned and chosen by persons who are formally enrolled as members of the Democratic Party of the United States. For all these reasons, there is little doubt that if the proposed charter or anything like it is adopted, it will no longer be accurate to describe the national party, as most scholars have in the past, in terms like "a ghost party" or "a loose alliance of [state and local parties] to win . . . the presidency."[68]

Of course it remains to be seen what the Democrats will do and to what extent the Republicans will follow suit. But the history of party reform in America shows that when one party makes a major change in its institutions, sooner or later the other party feels compelled to follow suit. Accordingly, if the federal courts allow the national parties to rule their own affairs, I find it hard to believe that either the Democrats or the Republicans will ever revert to the nearly complete decentralization which, prior to the 1950s, made them both so unlike any other major party in the Western world.

[68] The first phrase is Schattschneider's, and the second is from Arthur W. Macmahon, in E. R. A. Seligman and A. Johnson (eds.), *Encyclopaedia of the Social Sciences* (New York: The Macmillan Company, 1933), Vol. XI, p. 596.

CHAPTER SIX

Getting What We Want

Political scientists make their living by commenting on other people's political ideas and actions, as I have done in this book, Some, however, occasionally sally forth from classroom and library to become political actors themselves, as I did from 1969 to 1972 by participating in the McGovern-Fraser commission. When that happens, the political scientist risks becoming a subject of comment—and learning the hard way how different that is from being a commentator. This is only elementary justice, of course; but the learning experience may not be unmixed joy.

Thus, as a longstanding admirer of Theodore H. White's books on how America chooses its Presidents, I read with some disquiet the following passage from his volume on the 1972 election:

It was Austin Ranney, professor of political science at the University of Wisconsin, who set the quota idea in motion, though before the day was out, and consistently ever since, he has expressed his abhorrence of quotas. The transcript of the meeting reads:

RANNEY: . . .our fellow black Democrats feel that something more is needed than a no discrimination rule. . . . I want to suggest. . .that the

Commission at the very least urge. . .that there be included as members of the delegation, adequate, fair, whatever the word may be, representation of minority groups in the population.

. . . [Later] others had begun to feel that the same guarantee given blacks should be given to women and youth. Chief among those who wanted to extend categorical enfranchisement to the two other groups was Fred Dutton, one of the party's leading political theorists, and later one of McGovern's senior strategists.

DUTTON: There is no reason why our national convention shouldn't have 50% women, 10 or 15% young people.

Others supported Dutton's proposal, chiefly the three women on the commission, none of them by any means radical, but fighting for their bloc, as women, to get what the blacks had won.

Perhaps the most lucid critic of what was going on was the commission's second academic member, Professor Samuel Beer of Harvard's Department of Government.

BEER: I'd like to speak out against Fred Dutton's proposal. . . .what we're doing here is usurping the function of the voters themselves. . . . It's not for us to say to the voters of a state you've got to elect 50% women. If the voters want 75% women or 75% men, it's up to them. . . . I think it would be a great mistake and would make us look really ridiculous and would never work if we tried to say that you must have proportionate representation of young people and women in your conventions.

DUTTON: . . .As far as the idea being ridiculous, I can't think of anything more attractive

or a better way to get votes with media politics
than to have half of that convention floor in 1972
made up of women. . . .we're talking about winning elections, we've got to provide the symbols.
. .which will activate women. . .activate young
people, which will appeal to them, and this is a
tangible device for doing just that.
. . .RANNEY [who had now changed from his
earlier insistence on something strong to force the
inclusion of blacks]: I have the feeling, with
Senator Bayh's assistance, I opened Pandora's
box here. . . . I think we ought to recognize [that]
if we pass this motion now we're going to a quota
system. . . . How can we. . .give proportional
representation to political views while making
sure that there is adequate representation of
blacks, women, youth. . . ?[1]

As a participant-observer in these events, I have some
observations about White's observations about my participation. For one, his account of what happened is correct.
I *did*, however short-sightedly, start the commission
toward the quotas morass by advocating some kind of
guarantee for more representation of black Democrats in
future conventions. I did not foresee that the same guarantees would be demanded for women and youth, and I
agreed (and still agree) with commissioner Will Davis that
"we don't have any evidence at all like we have in the
black situation of discrimination against either women or
youth because of the fact that they are women or young."[2]
When I realized that the claims of all three groups would

---

[1] Theodore H. White, *The Making of the President 1972* (New York:
Atheneum, 1973), pp. 29-31. Elisions within the quotations are White's;
elisions between the quotations are mine.
[2] *Ibid.*, p. 31.

be pressed as a single package, I recognized, belatedly, that I had "opened Pandora's box," and joined the other commissioners who were trying to resist all quotas. But it was too late, and, as White records, we lost.

Even so, this humbling experience was not a total loss for me. My failures as a political actor at least added a good deal of reinforcement to a conclusion I have reached as a scholar in this book and elsewhere. Briefly stated, it is the conviction that the actual consequences of party reform are, in the future as in the past, likely often to disappoint their advocates, relieve their opponents, and surprise a lot of commentators.

This conclusion is admittedly a muted note on which to end this book, but I believe there are good reasons for holding it. One is that no political scientist or party leader or political journalist enjoys more than a limited and imperfect ability to forecast the consequences of adopting particular reform proposals. Another is that most party reformers *and* their opponents, like most Americans, have ambivalent feelings about just how the parties should be organized and fitted into our system of governance. And a third is that even if we knew exactly how to get the kind of parties we want, which we do not, we would still disagree about the kind of parties to establish and the prices worth paying for them.

Let us examine all three propositions in detail.

MAKING EVERYBODY HAPPY

Suppose some Edison or Marconi of political science were to perfect political engineering to the point where we knew just how to write our rules so as to establish exactly the party organizations and processes we wanted. Would we then end the two centuries of quarreling described in this book and agree at last on which reforms to adopt or reject? I doubt it very much; for this book's basic thesis is that Americans, now as always, have ambivalent feelings about whether political parties are basically malignant or benign and about how they should be organized and fitted to our governing system to do the most good or the least harm. This ambivalence seems to me just as widespread among the nation's political and academic elites as among its mass publics. And I believe that for elites and masses alike party reform continues to offer what it has always offered: a welcome escape from the unhappy alternatives of abolishing parties or allowing them to act as they will. If this is correct, then whatever course party reform may take cannot possibly make everybody happy.

The same is true of the conclusions of this book. It should now be clear that the issues of party reform are bound up with some of the most fundamental, difficult, and unresolved issues of political theory. Both as a political scientist and a quondam political reformer I have views on them; but I am well aware, as the reader should be, that other scholars and political activists hold different views. Let us consider some of the leading issues in point.

PARTISAN SUCCESS AND ORGANIZATIONAL PURITY

Even a faithful Green Bay Packers fan finds it hard to subscribe unreservedly to the late Vince Lombardi's dictum that "winning is not the main thing; it is the only thing." That, after all, was the Watergate conspirators' excuse for their crimes, and it is a moral stance deadly for fair or democratic government. Accordingly, in evaluating any proposal for party reform even the most devoted party or candidate enthusiast should ask: Is it fair? It is moral?

Yet, as a partisan, it seems to me also that winning elections is a necessary if not sufficient condition for achieving whatever goals my party has; and I cannot reasonably deny the same premise to my counterparts in the other party. Consequently, we partisans must also ask of each reform proposal: will it help or hurt our party's chances to win elections? I remember, in this regard, a principle expounded by one of my first political science teachers. It takes many qualities to make a great President of the United States, he said; but the *first* quality it takes is the ability to get nominated and elected. If a person has all the other qualities but that one, his other virtues will not matter, for he will never be President.

This still rings true, and I take it to mean that if my party's presidential nominating rules are such as consistently to produce losers, then they are bad rules however they may seem to satisfy abstract canons of equity, representativeness, and the like. That seems to me to have its own morality: not all means effective for achieving good ends are good, but all means *in*effective for achieving good ends are bad. Yet there is no denying that many of my fellow partisans—especially the "purists" discussed in Chapter 4—are devoted to a more generalized version of Henry Clay's famous preference for being right over being President. I do not expect that, in my party at least, either view will ever entirely persuade or dominate the other.

PARTY MEMBERSHIP AND INTRAPARTY DEMOCRACY

In my judgment, Americans have paid a considerable price for their almost boundaryless conceptions and permissive legal definitions of party membership, as described in Chapter 5. E.E. Schattschneider pointed out decades ago that the prevalence of these notions has made inevitable the repeated attacks on the party organizations as unrepresentative and oligarchical, and has led to the recurring efforts to "democratize" them by such devices as replacing caucuses with conventions and conventions with direct primaries. Since only a small fraction of the citizenry are concerned enough with internal party affairs to participate in these "democratized" structures, Schattschneider argued, such reforms are bound to disappoint their advocates and, what is worse, intensify the widespread belief that parties are by their very nature oligarchical and evil. He concluded:

> A more realistic theory, closer to the facts, can relieve us of the nightmarish necessity of doing the impossible. Let us suppose that the concept of the party membership of the partisans is abandoned altogether. If the party is described as a political enterprise conducted by a group of working politicians *supported* by partisan voters who approve of the party but are merely partisans (not members of a fictitious association), the parties would seem less wicked.[3]

Since Schattschneider wrote these words, things have gotten worse from his point of view. More states have adopted and expanded the coverage of direct primaries. Since the late 1960s both major parties have tried to democratize their national conventions by increasing the influence of issue and candidate partisans over party regulars and officeholders. Even more than in Schattschneider's day, American parties are incontestably the most open and internally democratic in the world—*if*, that is, one accepts the notion that anyone who says he is a party member should be treated as one.

[3] E.E. Schattschneider, *Party Government* (New York: Farrar and Rinehart, 1942), p. 59, emphasis in the original.

Yet have these changes made our parties better instruments of democratic government than, say, the much more closed parties in other Western democracies? The leading scholar of comparative parties replies, in effect: different, yes; better, no.[4] And some commentators continue to press the responsible-party-government doctrine that what America needs is more unified, disciplined, programmatic parties, not looser and more fragmented parties, even if the latter are in some sense more representative. They agree with Schattschneider's view that "democracy is not to be found *in* the parties but *between* the parties."[5]

But their cause has not prospered in recent years. All of the new reforms—especially the McGovern-Fraser guidelines, the DO committee rules, and the expansion of presidential primaries—have sought wider participation and better representation, not closer cohesion and tighter discipline.[6] So it seems likely that conflict over party reform, at least in the 1970s, will center mainly on issues of who should be represented in party councils and how.

FAIR CONTESTS AND QUOTA-GUARANTEED OUTCOMES

My political activities no less than my academic studies have convinced me of two lessons relevant for our present concerns. First, real-life political decisions are rarely choices between flawless goods and unmitigated evils; they are usually choices between one good thing and another. Second, making such choices is often so difficult and painful that the choosers try to have it both ways.

[4] Cf. Leon D. Epstein, *Political Parties in Western Democracies* (New York: Frederick A. Praeger, 1967), pp. 111-129.

[5] *Op. cit.*, p. 60, emphasis in the original.

[6] In addition to the reports of the McGovern-Fraser commission and the DO committee, the leading manifesto for more participatory democracy in the parties is John S. Saloma III and Frederick H. Sontag, *Parties: The Real Opportunity for Effective Citizen Politics* (New York: Random House Vintage Books, 1973).

Curing the Mischiefs of Faction

Clearly this is what happened in the McGovern-Fraser commission's agonies over the issue of how to make Democratic national conventions more representative. Nearly all of us wanted more faithful "preferential representation," and so we sought a convention composed of delegations whose distributions of presidential preferences accurately reflected the distributions of preferences among the "rank-and-file Democrats" in their respective states and territories. But the commission's majority also wanted, and got, "demographic representation": a convention of delegations whose distributions of minority ethnic group members, women, and young people would bear a "reasonable relationship to their presence in the population of the State."

As a result, the 1972 convention was a hodgepodge of representative inconsistencies. It closely approached full representation-by-quotas for blacks, women, and youth—but greatly underrepresented the elderly, the poor, the white ethnics, and labor union members, to say nothing of the party's senators, congressmen, governors, and other notables. Nearly two-thirds of the convention's delegates were chosen or bound by presidential primaries; but 57 percent of its first-ballot votes and the nomination went to a candidate who had won only 27 percent of the popular votes cast in the primaries and who had only 30 percent of the first-choice preference's in Gallup's last preconvention poll of Democrats.[7]

Thus, guaranteeing quota representation for blacks, women, and young people did not come free. One cost was the substantial underrepresentation of other demographic groups also important to the party and the nation. An even greater cost, in my view, was the damage done

[7] The convention balloting is given in *Congressional Quarterly Weekly Report.* July 15, 1972, p. 1720; the results of the presidential primaries are listed in July 8, 1972, p. 1655; the Gallup Poll is reported in July 15, 1972, p. 1778.

to the competing principle of preferential representation. Quite aside from any consideration of how the new nominating procedures might have affected the party's fortunes in November, it seems to me the costs of the demographic quotas were far too high for whatever benefits, if any, they may have brought the party, the nation, or even the favored groups. I am pleased that the Mikulski commission and the Democratic National Committee have outlawed such quotas in selecting delegates for the 1976 convention, although it remains to be seen whether the new rule for "affirmative action" will result in de facto quotas.

CONFRONTATION AND ACCOMMODATION

I am well aware that many of the most idealistic and politically active Americans believe that the prime obligations of a political party are to develop a clear and far-reaching policy program, to proclaim it vigorously, and to implement it fully when the party wins power. The corollary is that the collective obligation of all the parties competing in our system or any other is to present the voters with unequivocal and substantially different programs. Only thus, it is argued, can the voters have truly meaningful choices; and only thus will elections be what they should be: unambiguous confrontations between genuine antagonists resulting in clearcut victories for the party with the strongest popular support.

Many people of widely differing ideologies have long pressed this view. To be sure, they have disagreed about which party and program would or should win such confrontations; but they have all agreed that sharpening differences and posing clear choices should be the main function of our party system. Moreover, this function should provide the principal criterion for judging all party reform proposals.

It is not surprising, therefore, that one of the oldest and most persistent indictments of American parties is that they "do not stand for anything," either ideologically or programmatically, and consequently do not offer the voters "a real choice." Lord Bryce launched the attack for academics with his observation that the Democrats and Republicans are "two bottles, each having a label denoting the kind of liquor it contains, but each being empty."[8] As every lecturer on parties knows, quoting this remark is still guaranteed to win laughter and approving nods from many audiences, especially college classes. And its message is still repeated by adherents of many different political ideologies and movements.

For example, the New Left: the 1962 Port Huron Statement of the nascent Students for a Democratic Society declared that "a crucial feature of the political apparatus in America is that greater differences are harbored within each major party than the differences between them instead of two parties presenting distinctive and significant differences of approach. . . ."[9]

For another example, the Old Left: the 1966 *New* Program of the Communist Party U.S.A. states:

As contained within the institutionalized two-party framework the old alignment is an intricate barrier to clearcut confrontation of conflicting economic and social interests. It thus confounds a genuine national debate on fundamental issues, and such debate as does develop is precluded from serving the function of

[8] James Bryce, *The American Commonwealth* (rev. ed., New York: Macmillan, 1911), Vol. II, p. 29.

[9] Reprinted in Paul Jacobs and Saul Landau, *The New Radicals: A Report with Documents* (New York: Random House Vintage Books, 1966), p. 160. For a more detailed and sophisticated exposition of this view, see David Schuman, *A Preface to Politics* (Lexington, Mass.: D.C. Heath, 1973), pp. 84-85.

presenting a democratic choice between the most meaningful political alternatives.[10]

But the Right is no less devoted to the confrontation ideal. In 1964, for example, the La Passionara of the Goldwater conservative movement, Phyllis Schlafly, declared that Republican presidential candidates had never provided the voters with "a choice not an echo," and it was high time they did. For, she argued,

> America is best served when the two great political parties compete with one another to the fullest possible extent consistent with ethical conduct. . . . Like trials, political campaigns should be competitive and adversarial.[11]

And George Wallace's third-party movement in 1968 was founded on his often-proclaimed conviction that "there's not a dime's worth of difference in any of 'em, national Democrats or national Republicans."[12]

The least shrill and, to me, most impressive statements of this indictment have been made by a series of distinguished political scientists, numbering such great names as Woodrow Wilson, Frank J. Goodnow, Stephen K. Bailey, and, above all, E.E. Schattschneider.[13] In recent years its most eloquent advocate has been their eminent successor, James MacGregor Burns. He lays it right on the line:

[10] *NEW Program of the Communist Party U.S.A. (A Draft)* (New York: Political Affairs Publishers, 1966), p. 76; the emphasis in the title is in the original.

[11] Phyllis Schlafly, *A Choice Not An Echo* (Alton, Ill.: Pere Marquette Press, 1964), pp. 28-29.

[12] Quoted in Lewis Chester, Godfrey Hodgson and Bruce Page, *An American Melodrama* (New York: Dell, 1969), p. 313.

[13] Their views are discussed in many places, including my *The Doctrine of Responsible Party Government* (Urbana, Ill.: University of Illinois Press, 1954, 1962), Chs. 2-6.

Curing the Mischiefs of Faction

We lack popular control of the policy-making process. Our splintered parties set up barriers between the people and their national government rather than simplifying the alternatives, clarifying competing party doctrines, and allowing the victorious majority to govern.[14]

But Americans seldom speak with one voice on any issue, and this is no exception. Another, equally distinguished, succession of political analysts have argued that the parties should give first priority to a very different function. They have taken the view that, in America at least, the first obligation of our institutions must be to manage the hot competition among our many interests in such a way that it will be conducted peacefully and avoid total victory or total defeat for any competitor. Americans, they believe, are all too easily committed to such warlike political objectives as the opposition's "unconditional surrender" and are all too ready to use violence to get it. Political parties can and must play a major role in restraining the application of these dangerous attitudes to the conduct of our politics.

But how? Mainly, they say, as a side effect of the parties' efforts to put together winning electoral and legislative coalitions. They contend that if each major party sought victory by total commitment to the interests of some Americans and—the necessary reciprocal—by total rejection of others' interests, then each would champion one part of the nation against another in a political *guerre à outrance* whose verdict the losers could not and would

[14] James MacGregor Burns, *The Deadlock of Democracy* (rev. ed., Englewood Cliffs, N.J. Prentice-Hall, 1963), p. 324. Similar views are set forth in Harvey Wheeler, *The Restoration of Politics* (Santa Barbara, Calif.: Center for the Study of Democratic Institutions, 1965), and David S. Broder, *The Party's Over* (New York: Harper and Row, 1972).

not accept peacefully. In fact, however, each party has sought winning coalitions by attempting accommodations among competing interests it hopes will appeal to more contributors and voters than will the rival accommodations offered by the opposition party. This strategy, it is conceded, has resulted in vague, ambiguous, and overlapping party programs and in elections that offer the voters choices between personalities and, at most, general programmatic tendencies, certainly not unequivocal choices between sharply different programs. But this, they believe, is not a vice but a virtue, for it has enabled Americans through all but one era of their history to manage their differences with relatively little violence and to preserve the world's oldest constitutional democratic regime. Even the one great exception is held to support this thesis: the parties tried longer and harder than the churches or the universities or any other institution to resolve the issues of slavery and secession without civil war; and after Appomattox they more than any other institution helped to put the nation back together.[15]

In weighing the merits of this issue, I realize that not every American feels that the Civil War was our worst political failure or that avoiding another one should be our first concern. Some no doubt would point to the Vietnam war, others to "creeping socialism," others to white racism, others to male chauvinism, others to Watergate, others to the New Deal. But I confess that Sir Denis Brogan was talking about people like me when he wrote:

Although it may be rash to suggest a belief in a national memory, it is at any rate possible that the

[15] For the efforts of the parties, particularly the Democrats, to prevent the war, see Roy F. Nichols, *The Disruption of American Democracy* (New York: Macmillan, 1948). For the parties' role in reconstruction, see Paul H. Buck, *The Road to Reunion* (Boston: Little, Brown, 1937), and C. Vann Woodward, *Reunion and Reaction* (Boston: Little, Brown, 1951).

American shrinking. from doctrinaire parties, from
people who knew their own minds, who would not
compromise, who had a social theory to defend or
attack, owed something to the recollection of the time
when America *had* such parties, when, to the aston-
ishment of each side, North and South found themselves at war.[16]

A balance of probable costs against probable benefits
favoring accommodation over confrontation seemed sensible to me even in what now seems the bovine placidity
of the Eisenhower era.[17] It has seemed even more sensible
in the far more acrimonious, violent, and dangerous era
of Kennedy, Johnson, and Nixon. Yes, we system-defend-
ers *were* a bit smug in the 1950s. We thought the American
political system was working better than any the world
had ever seen, and I suppose we assumed it always would.
The assassinations, ghetto riots, violent protests, "White
House horrors" and "dirty tricks" of the 1960s and 1970s
have certainly stripped the smugness from all of us and
even hope from some of us. But, to me at least, these
awful events have taught not only how fragile is the politics
of accommodation and civility but also how precious it
is and how worthy of our best efforts to preserve it.

In the end, however, the issue will be settled more by
ordinary Americans than by intellectuals. So it is important to ask again, as we did in Chapter 2: do Americans
want a politics of confrontation or a politics of accommodation? The data presented in Chapter 2 suggest that they

[16] D.W. Brogan, *Politics in America* (rev. ed., New York: Harper
Torchbooks, 1969), p. 54, emphasis in the original.

[17] See, for example, Austin Ranney and Willmoore Kendall, *Democracy and the American Party System* (New York: Harcourt, Brace,
1956), esp. pp. 527-533. My views, then and now, owe much to the
analyses in Pendleton Herring, *The Politics of Democracy* (New York:
W.W. Norton, 1940, reprinted in 1965); and Herbert Agar, *The Price
of Union* (Boston: Houghton Mifflin, 1950).

want *both*—sort of.[18] Most of them agree that "the parties do more to confuse the issues than to provide a clear choice on them," that "our senators and representatives ought to follow their parties more than they do," and that "democracy works best where competition between the parties is strong." But most of them also believe that "the conflicts and controversies between the parties hurt our country more than they help it," that "the political parties more often than not create conflicts where none really exists," and even that "our system of government would work a lot more efficiently if we could get rid of conflicts between the parties altogether." Presented with the most clearly confrontationist proposition that "things would be better if the parties took opposite stands on issues more than they do now," 31 percent agreed, 43 percent disagreed, and the rest had mixed feelings or no opinion.

These statements, remember, were presented to Wisconsin adults in November and December of 1964 and have not been presented since in a sample survey. But I find it hard to believe that if they felt this way about the politics of Lyndon Johnson, Barry Goldwater, and Martin Luther King they would now be more eager for sharp choices and confrontations after having lived through the politics of Richard Nixon, George McGovern, and Mark Rudd.

HOPES, FEARS, AND SURPRISES

REFORMS AND RESULTS

The preceding chapters have shown that the events since 1968 are only the most recent of many reminders that party rules and practices are far from being fixed and immutable. If the time is ripe, as it was in the late 1820s,

[18] See Table 3, p. 55.

the early 1900s, and the late 1960s, then party rules can be changed quickly and even radically. In such times, indeed, the advocates of almost any reform appear to have more élan—and a better press—than their opponents. The whole zeitgeist seems to support the feeling that, while some reforms may be better than others, any reform is better than no reform at all.

But party reforms, like all political actions, have consequences. And the events described earlier in the book have shown that those consequences are often very different from those wished by reformers or feared by their opponents. The point is readily illustrated by a quick review of the main episodes we have considered.

In the first episode, the congressional caucus's monopoly over presidential nominations was broken in 1824 by men who sought to keep William Crawford out of the presidency, to end congressional domination of the executive, and to establish state control of the national parties. They achieved all their goals, but they soon encountered new difficulties to which establishing national conventions seemed the answer. The conventions were intended to be the creatures of the state parties, and that is what they became. But one unexpected and often unwelcome result was the frequent deadlocks that could be broken only by passing over prominent national leaders and choosing such little-known and uninspiring compromises as James K. Polk, Franklin Pierce, Alton B. Parker, Warren G. Harding, and John W. Davis.

The second episode saw disgust with political corruption in the 1870s lead to elaborate legal codes regulating party structures and procedures from the 1880s on. Even so, corruption has somehow survived and, in some respects, gotten worse. The codes have been augmented from the 1920s to the present by an avalanche of state and national laws regulating campaign finance. Yet the appalling Watergate revelations of 1974 exposed a kind of corruption many people, including me, regard as more immoral and more destructive of democratic processes than any other in history. After all, the "White House horrors" were perpetrated not because our laws were inadequate but because some Nixon zealots believed that his reelection was so lofty an end that it justified using any means—including burglary, espionage, and sabotage. And it is important to remember that these criminal zealots operated entirely outside of, and sometimes expressed contempt for, their candidate's party. It therefore seems as pointless today as in previous eras to pass new laws requiring people to obey the laws already on the books.

In the third episode, Robert M. La Follette led the movement for the most radical party reform of all, the direct primary. He and many, though not all, of his Progressive supporters believed the reform would improve the parties' ability to mobilize behind progressive policies because nominations would no longer be made by "bosses" interested only in patronage. But the direct primary has had many unforeseen consequences: it has made each party candidate's nomination depend solely on the approval of those voters who happen to vote in his party's district primary. If they like him, it matters little how much the party leaders dislike him or how often he bolts the party's program; indeed, the voters may give him special approval for his "independence." So one result of the direct primary has been to make our parties even more decentralized and undisciplined than before and therefore even less capable of uniting behind any program, progressive or otherwise.

In the most recent episode, the McGovern-Fraser commission expected to achieve several worthy goals—and received some rude shocks after the guidelines were implemented. For one example, most of the commissioners strongly preferred a reformed national convention to a national presidential primary or a major increase in the number of state presidential primaries. And we believed that if we made the party's nonprimary delegate selection processes more open and fair, participation in them would increase greatly and consequently the demand for more primaries would fade away. But quite the opposite has happened. Since 1969 no fewer than eight states have newly adopted primaries, and in 1976 nearly 70 percent of all the delegates will be chosen or bound by them, as compared with less than half in 1968 and before. Moreover, Congress is now considering a national primary more seriously than ever before.

Of course, it cannot be said that the guidelines were the sole or main cause for the sudden increase in the number of primaries. But we do know that in a majority of the eight states the state Democratic parties, who controlled the governorships and both houses of the legislatures, decided that rather than radically revising their accustomed ways of conducting caucuses and conventions for other party matters it would be better to split off the process for selecting national convention delegates and let it be conducted by a state-administered primary which the national party would have to accept.

For another example, the commission's quota system was expected to produce much higher proportions of black, female, and young delegates and thus, as Frederick Dutton argued in the passage quoted earlier, increase the party's support among black, female, and young voters. We observed in Chapter 4 that greater demographic proportionality was indeed achieved among the 1972 convention's delegates. But public opinion polls and the election results showed that the second objective was badly missed. The relevant facts are summarized in Table 6.

TABLE 6
VOTE BY DEMOGRAPHIC GROUPS IN THE 1968 AND 1972
PRESIDENTIAL ELECTIONS

	1968 percent for			1972 percent for		Change in Democrats' percent, 1968–72
Voting Group	Humphrey	Nixon	Wallace	McGovern	Nixon	
National	43.0	43.4	13.6	38	62	−5
Men	41	43	16	37	63	−4
Women	45	43	12	38	62	−7
White	38	47	15	32	68	−6
Non-white	85	12	3	87	13	+2
Professional & business	34	56	10	31	69	−3
White collar	41	47	12	36	64	−5
Manual	50	35	15	43	57	−7
Members of labor union families	56	29	15	46	54	−10
College	37	54	9	37	63	—
High school	42	43	15	34	66	−8
Grade school	52	33	15	49	51	−3
Under 30 years	47	38	15	48	52	+1
30–49 years	44	41	15	33	67	−11
50 years & older	41	47	12	36	64	−5

Source: The Gallup Opinion Index, December, 1972, p. 10.

Table 6 shows that among the three groups especially favored by the Democrats' new quota system, the party's presidential candidate did no more than hold his own with black voters and young voters, and lost support among women voters at an even greater rate than his overall decline from the 1968 candidate's performance. We cannot say to what extent the party's above-average loss among such traditional supporters as manual workers and labor union families was due to the quotas or to their being left out of the quotas; but we can hardly avoid the conclusion that the quotas helped little if at all with the voters whom they were supposed to attract in record numbers.

THE OPAQUE CRYSTAL BALL

The foregoing review, I believe, suggests that no one concerned with party reform has been able to forecast the consequences of particular changes with much accuracy or consistency. This has been equally true for opponents and advocates, and for participants, observers, *and* participant-observers. So it seems short-sighted for any of us to proclaim the short-sightedness of some of us.

But why is our crystal ball so opaque? Why have we encountered so many surprises, pleasant and unpleasant, from our reforms? The answer, I think, is that party rules and procedures constitute only one set of factors operating in a vast maelstrom of other triggering and contagion factors. Consequently, one of the most difficult problems facing the analyst who seeks to explain a past political event is to isolate the single or even the most important independent cause-effect chain from the myriad intersecting causes and effects that permeate every such event.

Let me offer just one example. Some commentators and politicians are now saying that the McGovern-Fraser rules made McGovern's 1972 nomination inevitable, and that his nomination in turn made inevitable the party's thundering defeat in the election. But surely that is far too simple an explanation of either event. Remember that Barry Goldwater's 1964 nomination by the Republicans was just as contrary to established expectations as was McGovern's success eight years later. Like McGovern, Goldwater was nominated mainly because a large army of issue-oriented amateurs dedicated to his ideology and cause outworked and outfought the "old pro's" supporting his opponents. And like McGovern, Goldwater proved that nominating politics are different from general election politics by his landslide loss in November. But *unlike* McGovern, Goldwater won his nomination under his party's old, unreformed rules. So it is clear that the old rules did not prevent Goldwater's nomination, and it seems unlikely that the new rules were the sole cause of McGovern's nomination.

All this illustrates the tough problems political scientists face in trying to explain past events. It explains why most of us stay away from such viscerally satisfying simple declarations as "A caused B" and confine ourselves to such more colorless—but more candid and defensible—statements as, "There is X probability that A explains Y percent of the variance in B." And I do not need to labor the point that plausibly explaining the causes of past events is a good deal easier than accurately forecasting the consequences of present proposals and the course of future events.

MANIPULATING THE MANIPULABLE

Given all these uncertainties, then, why are so many political activists, today as often in the past, so worked up about pending proposals to change party rules and procedures? No doubt there are many reasons, but at least one is clear. Of all the many factors that affect the fate of candidates, factions, policies, and programs, party rules are the most easily manipulated. After all, a person who, say, longs to see his party controlled by dedicated liberals can have little effect upon the nation's demographic composition or the slow tides of public opinion or the course of labor union policies. But he *can* join a party reform movement and, as we have seen repeatedly in this book, have a good chance of getting the party's rules changed.

True, the results may not be all he had hoped for and may even include some he did not want at all. Yet the new rules will produce *some* change. And he can, with justice, tell himself that at least he is not meekly submitting to forces beyond his control or merely grumbling about how bad things are; he is *doing* something to make them better.

Viewed in this light, party reform is one of the easier forms of social engineering; and faith in social engineering has long been one of the dominant elements in the culture of America's political activists. That culture features, among other beliefs, the convictions that for every evil there is a remedy, that inaction in the face of evil is immoral, that if you cannot do everything you should at least do what you can, and that if you make mistakes now you can always correct them later. So long as such ideas continue to play a major role in how politically active Americans approach political problems, efforts to reform the parties will be as prominent in our future as they have been in our past.

As a liberal Democrat and sometime party reformer, I have shared that culture and acted accordingly. But as a political scientist I should conclude by reminding all who seek political salvation through party reform of Ralph Waldo Emerson's wise aphorism: "The sower may mistake and sow his peas crookedly; the peas make no mistake but come up and show his line."[19]

[19] In W.H. Gilman and J.E. Parsons (eds.), *The Journals and Miscellaneous Notebooks of Ralph Waldo Emerson* (Cambridge, Mass.: Belknap Press of Harvard University Press, 1970), Vol. VIII, p. 398, journal entry of May 18, 1843.

Index

Index

Index

215

"At a time when party reform is again in high gear, this carefully reasoned analysis by a noted political scientist and sometime party reformer should be required reading for political activists."

—*Library Journal*

James Madison's warning that the first objective of any republican government must be the search for "Methods of curing the mischiefs of faction" provides the launching point for Austin Ranney's review of the theory and practice of party reform in America. Focusing on the three main periods of reform, 1820-1840, 1890-1920, and 1956 to the present, Mr. Ranney argues that party rules and procedures have never been politically neutral and he describes what candidates and factions won and lost from each of the major reforms. He shows that Americans in all periods of our history, including the present, have had ambivalent feelings about the institution of parties, some wishing to abolish them, others wishing to leave them alone, but most wishing neither. The author's main thesis is that reform has always offered such people, and continues to offer them, a convenient escape from the difficult choice of abolishing parties or smoothing their way.

"Ranney . . . is considered one of the most penetrating commentators on American party politics. His work combines a deep understanding of the working of a two-party system in a complexly divided nation and a continuing preoccupation with the effects on democracy of different possible ways of organizing political parties. . . . Presented with clarity, perspective, and fluency in a way that makes the book . . . must reading for students of American parties."

—*Choice*

"This is an important book. . . . Dr. Ranney, a member of the McGovern-Fraser Commission which wrote the Democratic Party guidelines, is my candidate to write the post-1976 election analysis."

—*Christian Science Monitor*

University of California Press   Berkeley 94720